Practices of Selfhood

Practices of Selfhood

Zygmunt Bauman &
Rein Raud

polity

Copyright © Zygmunt Bauman and Rein Raud 2015

The right of Zygmunt Bauman and Rein Raud to be identified as Author of this Work has been asserted in accordance with the UK Copyright, Designs and Patents Act 1988.

First published in 2015 by Polity Press

Polity Press
65 Bridge Street
Cambridge CB2 1UR, UK

Polity Press
350 Main Street
Malden, MA 02148, USA

ISBN-13: 978-0-7456-9016-2
ISBN-13: 978-0-7456-9017-9(pb)

A catalogue record for this book is available from the British Library.

Library of Congress Cataloging-in-Publication Data

Bauman, Zygmunt, 1925-
    Practices of selfhood / Zygmunt Bauman, Rein Raud.
        pages cm
    Includes bibliographical references and index.
    ISBN 978-0-7456-9016-2 (hardback : alk. paper) – ISBN 978-0-7456-9017-9 (pbk. :
alk. paper) 1. Self (Philosophy) 2. Self. 3. Group identity. 4. Civilization,
Modern–21st century. I. Raud, Rein. II. Title.
    BD450.B358 2015
    126–dc23
                        2014035818

Typeset in 11/13 Sabon
by Toppan Best-set Premedia Limited
Printed and bound in the United Kingdom by CPI Group (UK) Ltd, Croydon, CRO 4YY

For further information on Polity, visit our website:
politybooks.com

Contents

Preface

We first conceived the idea of this book during a winter school at Tallinn University, where Zygmunt was the keynote speaker and Rein one of the heads of the programme committee. One of the events of that school was a discussion between us, open to the public, on many topics touched also in this book. The hour allocated to that conversation was, of course, far from sufficient and thus it continued over dinner and then migrated into our correspondence, soon taking on a more structured shape and organizing all the ideas that have been intriguing both of us along a central core, a concept that we believe to be of fundamental importance to any discussion of the present world – that of selfhood.

How does an individual understand her or his position in the world? Are we determined by our genetic heritage, social circumstances and cultural preferences – and only tricked into believing that we make our own choices? By whom? Other individuals who have been determined similarly? Or are we autonomous – wholly or partly – and, if so, then to what degree? Are we or are we not autonomous enough to control and change the legacy fate has landed us with? How does selfhood emerge? Does it follow the same pattern of development in all people, all cultures, all ages? Or is it itself a socio-cultural construction that should be viewed in its historical context? If so, then what is happening right now – are the patterns of selfhood changing in the present world? Does contemporary technology allow us more autonomy – or does it tempt us to give up the freedoms we have?

A host of questions... All the dilemmas from which they arise could be plotted on the same axis – one end of which is designated by fate and determination and the other by choice and freedom. Notwithstanding the huge library of social and psychological studies these questions have inspired and continue to inspire, very few of them, if any, evoke obvious (and above all reliable, let alone definitive) answers. Possibly with good reason – some questions are important precisely for the ongoing dialogue they generate. All the same, fundamental as they are 'to any discussion of the present world' and also to awareness of the place in the world assigned to or earned by its inhabitants as well as their ability (or its lack) to change their lot, people struggling with their environment yearn for precisely such answers. This is why we felt the need to revisit the theories of self on offer in various places and cultural traditions, surveying their encouraging and disappointing potentials, and occasionally to pinpoint some insufficiently explored tracts or to suggest – even if tentatively – some new and as yet untrodden paths worth following. Needless to say, all the time we remained aware that final, definite, foolproof answers are utterly unlikely to be found or composed; and that the main cause of their evasiveness lies not so much in the (temporary and reparable) insufficiency of our knowledge as in the nature of the world we inhabit – as well as our human, all too human, mode of inhabiting it.

To put it in a nutshell: popular wisdom insists that to know means to control, oblivious to the fact that the controlling power of knowledge depends on its ability to predict with certainty the effects of our actions; the snag, though, is that our world is anything but certain. For better or worse, uncertainty is our fate: for worse, because uncertainty is an un-drying fount of our misery, and for better, because it is also the prime cause of our glory – of human inventiveness, creativity, and our capacity of transcending one by one the limits it sets to human potential.

One way to look at the situation is suggested to us by the studies of Nobel Prize holder Ilya Prigogine, a great natural scientist as well as a philosopher of science. The gist of his message is best conveyed in his reminder that 'Obviously when fish came to earth not all fish came to earth. When monkeys became human, not all monkeys became human' (2003: 64). This, in optimally condensed form, summarizes the worldview prompted by 'the end of certainty' and its consequences for modern science.

'Classical science emphasized order and stability; now, in contrast, we see fluctuation, instability, multiple choices, and limited predictability at all levels of observation' (Prigogine 1997: 4). According to classical science, probabilities were 'states of [ignorant or insufficiently informed] mind rather than states of the world'. However, 'once probabilities are included in the formulation of the basic laws of physics, the future is no longer determined by the present' (1997: 6); accordingly, science itself can no longer claim absolute certainty, nor can probability be identified with ignorance (1997: 7). 'The future is no longer given', Prigogine concludes; 'Our world is a world of continuous "construction" ruled by probabilistic laws and no longer a kind of automaton. We are led from a world of "being" to a world of "becoming"' (2003: 39). In other words: for most practical intents and purposes, the condition of 'uncertainty' has been shifted from the realm of epistemology (the study of cognition) to that of ontology (the study of being).

And, to cut a long story short: we now know, understand and believe that the non-attainability of certainty, as well as the impossibility of predicting the future other than in probability terms is not an effect of the dearth of knowledge, but of the excessive, principally unlimited, complexity of the universe. The history of humans as much as the history of universe needs to be retold in terms of 'events' – something not-inevitable, underdetermined; something that might but also might not happen. Let us repeat what needs to be recognized, reconciled to, and permanently kept in our minds: history is *not* given before it turns into the present (that means, reaching the moment of its recycling into the past); it is instead, as Prigogine insists, 'under perpetual construction' – as much as the history of any individual, namely 'biography'.

The bold – or rather, arrogant – conviction of Pierre-Simon de Laplace that 'once we know the initial conditions, we can calculate all subsequent states as well as the preceding ones' (Prigogine 1997: 11), can no longer be sustained – and this applies as much to the states of the universe as to the states of individual humans. As for the latter, Prigogine (1997: 186) cites an unpublished manuscript of Carl Rubino – 'For human men and women, for us, immutability, freedom from change, total security, immunity from life's maddening ups and downs, will come only when we depart this life, by dying, or becoming gods.' And comments: 'Odysseus is fortunate enough to be given the choice between immortality, by remaining forever the lover of Calypso, and a return to humanity and ultimately old age and death. In the end, he chooses time over eternity, human fate over the fate of the gods.' Jorge Luis Borges, an exquisitely sublime practitioner and theorist of *belles lettres* as well as one of the greatest philosophers of the human condition, serenely accepts the consequences of such a choice: 'Time is the substance of which I am made. Time is a river that sweeps me along, but I am the river; it is a tiger that mangles me, but I am the tiger; it is a fire that consumes me, but I am the fire. The world, unfortunately, is real; I, unfortunately, am Borges' (1999: 332).

What are the implications of Prigogine's scientific insights and Borges' eloquent statements on the human condition? Is it at all possible to speak with sense about something called 'selfhood' in a world where certainty, too, has been demystified? Where and when we no longer consider strict frameworks and streamlined processes the primary structural model for explaining anything? Perhaps it is indeed hopeless to proceed from a holistic vision of the human self to its particular manifestations in social and cultural practice. In any case, that is the assumption that has prompted us to move our conversation from topic to topic, from aspect to aspect, and to try to see how selfhood is brought together and taken apart in social practice, through language, through efforts of self-presentation, through programmatic attempts of self-realization – as well as, last but not least, through interaction with other selves.

Spelling out and trying to unpack the contents of the quandaries listed above have sometimes kept both of us up to the wee hours and checking emails first thing in the morning. Both reassurances and provocations have made us rethink our positions and prove, not only to each other but also to ourselves, that things we have considered obvious are indeed so – and sometimes discover that they are not. But this is what such dialogues are for. Presenting them to you, our readers, we hope that you enjoy them as much as we have enjoyed composing them.

Zygmunt Bauman
Rein Raud

1

Starting Out

Rein Raud In a sense, it could perhaps be said that the history of modernity is also a history of a certain type of self: the basically rational individual, the singular person in control of and answerable for her/his actions, capable of associating her-/himself with, or disassociating her-/himself from, larger communities and causes. But, for most of the time, modernity has also cherished a view of truth we might call scientific – that there must necessarily be a single, universal and objective truth out there – and therefore this view of human selfhood, too, has presented a claim to universality, a claim to characterize the way how people are and have been everywhere and throughout history. The variability of the idea of the self through time and between cultures of different types is a topic I'd like to come back to at a later moment. For now, could we perhaps try to diagnose the position of the self in the present world? Since Freud and Nietzsche, Western thought has also come a long way in abandoning the idea of a single, indivisible, self-contained and self-controlled individual. At least in theory. In our social practice, the view of what we are still seems to conform to a rather more simplistic concept of the individual as a political, economic and cultural subject. The word 'crisis' has obviously gone through a rather steep inflation, so I'm not going to talk about a 'crisis' of selfhood. But, at the same time, it still seems quite clear that under the circumstances of 'liquid modernity', to use your term, this inherited view of selfhood is no longer either adequate or functional.

Zygmunt Bauman   No disagreement here: indeed, the 'history of modernity' is also a history of 'a certain type of self'. But what kind of self? Or, rather, of what kind of its 'existential modality'? It is, in my view, the latter that changed radically with the advent of modernity.

I'd suggest that its modality underwent three seminal alterations, or in other words acquired three new, essentially modern, qualities. First, it became an object of attention, scrutiny and contemplation. Second, it has been set apart, as a subject, from the rest of perceived entities, which by the same token were cast as its objects. Third, it has simultaneously been promoted to the status of the primary, privileged object of that newly construed subject. Let us note that all those three properties, defining between themselves the 'modern self', were brought together and blended in Pico della Mirandola's 1486 manifesto recorded under the trailblazing title of the 'Oration on the Dignity of Man' and destined to turn into a self-fulfilling prophecy. The 'dignity' in that title has been unpacked in the 'Oration' as a status bringing to mind a sort of remarkable – and thoroughly unique – 'three in one, one in three' merger/union of a violinist, a violin, and the recipient and judge of the quality of pleasurable sounds which the violinist extracts from the violin.

The first new (modern) quality was, to deploy Martin Heidegger's distinction, a result of recasting the 'self' from the modality of *Zuhanden* into that of *Vorhanden*; from something given, too obvious to be paid any attention, indeed 'hidden in the light' of its obviousness, unnoticed and unproblematic – into a task: a challenge calling for close examination and needing to be studied in depth in order to be fully comprehended, tackled, dealt with, acted upon, revised, improved on; in short, as thoroughly and perpetually, endemically, problematic.

The second new quality found its seminal articulation in the Cartesian duo of subject and object. As a sensing, thinking, designing and acting subject, the 'self' transforms the rest of the world into an aggregate of passive objects of its sensations, thoughts, designs and actions. Descartes' *cogito* was more, much more than a short shrift to neo-Pyrrhonians, a declaration of self-confidence as well a legitimation of the self's truth-seeking ambitions; in a somewhat oblique yet no less resolute way, it was also an act of self's coronation: of perching the self at the peak of creation, endowed with the double prerogative of the supreme tribunal and the legislator-in-chief of truth – not only an artist capable of painting a faithful likeness of the world, but potentially also the chief engineer of the world whose truth is sought, explored and decreed. The *cogito* was calculated to lift the 'self' from its existential uncertainty, placate its existential anxiety, and to reverse the relation of mastery and dependence between the self as cognizing subject and the world, the object of its cognition.

The third novelty is the duty of the self's self-concern, self-creation, self-scrutiny and self-control. The subject itself has joined the ranks of the objects of the self's cognitive zeal, care and creative intervention. The supreme maker of things doubles in the role of the primary object of its making/remaking concerns. Socrates astonished, puzzled, nonplussed and embarrassed his fellow Athenians when suggesting that they ought to take care of their πνεῦμα (pneuma). They found this demand oxymoronic – but that contradiction in terms turned in the modern era into a no longer questioned life truth.

It was Cicero who coined, metaphorically, the concept of *cultura animi*. In the third quarter of the eighteenth century his idea was resurrected in France and, alongside English 'refinement' and German *Bildung*, entered into the core, canonical vocabulary of modern discourse, fast losing the memory of its metaphorical origins. What that concept conveyed was the message of the incompleteness of nature's work: humans are not *born* human, but *made* – in the incessant self-formation, self-assertion and self-improvement effort – all of them guided, directed, aided and abetted by the human community which they entered at birth.

RR I'd like to add a fourth characteristic to the status of the modern self – its relation to time. The medieval self had had to project itself against the background of eternity, as it were, and to be guided by considerations about the fate of the immortal soul. The modern self, while not immediately abandoning these concerns, still started to operate with a totally different timeframe. Perhaps we can say this happened as if in a film, when the focus shifts from the background to the hazy object in the foreground, and we start to see it clearly, but the background fades. Or, to use another, maybe more appropriate simile: the shutter speed changed. In a medieval painting, which depicts the life of a saint, we find it perfectly natural to see the same man in different places, because the painting represents his whole lifetime, still a mere moment compared to eternity. Not so in the modern painting from the Renaissance onwards, which is able to catch its actors in a momentary scene. Of course the self became more important if the coordinates that delimited its existence changed from eternity to something shorter, such as the lifespan of a single human being. What happened during that span acquired much more weight. But this also increased individual responsibility, and made the ideal of human dignity possible. Or *Bildung*. The ideal life of the previous period had been emulation, the repetition or enactment of a pre-existing matrix, something akin to Thomas à Kempis' *Imitation of Christ* (*c.*1427) – now, little by little, self-formation became the responsibility of the individual human being, something unrepeatable, totally her own. And it has stayed so to this day, even though the way selves are built has changed. I suppose this is a corollary of the idea of freedom, if we think of freedom as a state that characterizes one's being in society, and not just within one's mind.

> **ZB** When I consider the brief span of my life absorbed into the eternity which comes before and after – as the remembrance of a guest that tarrieth but a day (Wisdom V. 15.) – the small space I occupy and which I see swallowed up in the infinite immensity of space of which I know nothing and which knows nothing of me, I take fright and am amazed to see myself here rather than there, now rather than then. (Pascal 1966: 48)

So complained great Pascal in the name of his contemporaries. And he added: 'Man's greatness comes from knowing he is wretched, but there is greatness in knowing one is wretched.' 'Knowing, unlike any other living being, that we are mortal – and knowing it from the early moments of our lives', we are bound to live in the shadow of that knowledge. Living in its shadow, being aware of the laughable brevity of the life-span when compared with the eternity of the universe, and of the miserable minuteness of the place to which life will be confined if compared with the infinity of space, means knowing that 'there is no reason for me to be here rather than there, now rather than then'. 'No reason' equals 'no meaning'. But meaninglessness for a *Homo sapiens* is an unbearable condition. Human life is therefore an incessant effort to fill the appalling void, to *render life meaningful*; or – alternatively – either to forget life's existential meaninglessness or to suppress it, to declare it irrelevant, to play it down or to shift it onto a side burner and keep it there for the duration; in a nutshell, to make life-with-awareness-of-one's-own-mortality bearable – indeed, livable. That incessant effort we call *culture*. 'Culture' is another name for that greatness which Pascal spotted in our shared wretchedness.

You are right of course when pointing out that a new relation to time should be added as the fourth characteristic of the modern self – because we, moderns, have found a remedy for the suffering which Pascal lamented. I would even say, to strengthen your point, that seeking such remedies and finding them or deeming to have found them is the modern self's foremost trait – in as far as designing the ways of making life livable despite the awareness of mortality was, is, and probably will forever remain the main engine of culture and the common thread of its history. Modern ways of tackling that problem are indeed starkly distinct from the pre-modern.

I believe that the Christian solution was the most radical and indeed egalitarian of all alternative suggestions I can think of: according to Christianity, everyone had the prospect of eternity both guaranteed and inescapable (even if only in a spiritual form – as soul, not the body), but whether this immortality of soul would prove to be a blessing or a curse depended on the way the corporeal life was lived. This solution assigned to the brief episode of life-on-earth enormous significance of the only, not-to-be-repeated chance of influencing the *quality* of the eternal duration. (The pressure to do good and to avoid doing evil was in addition formidably strengthened by the concept of a hereditary original sin that set the stakes *a priori* in Hell's favour – everyone having been born already burdened with guilt; unless great effort was made to outweigh the awesome burden of original sin in the course of the earthly life, the chances of ending up in Hell outweighed those of reaching the Paradise.) The eternal fate of the immortal, indestructible soul could be influenced only during its captivity in the fleshy body – and would be decided there and then, once and for all. Once it lost its bodily carapace, there would be no chance to renegotiate its status and fate.

RR   There is certainly a connection between the Judaic immortal soul, accountable before a sole god, and the Western cultural gravitation towards individuality. But I wonder whether Christianity is really as radical as this. Of the three religions of the Book, perhaps Islam has developed this line of thought into a much more clear-cut, rational and non-negotiable version. As it is said in the Qur'ān: 'And among mankind is he who worshippeth God upon a narrow marge so that if good befalleth him he is content therewith, but if a trial befalleth him, he falleth away utterly. He loseth both the world and the Hereafter. That is the sheer loss' (22.11). The fall from grace, when it happens, is absolute, there is no way back, no matter how much one might then regret one's evil deed.

The achievement of Christianity, in my opinion, is exactly the opposite: it allows the individual basically to fail in everything, and still does not condemn the soul to eternal torture if it is really, really sorry for the bad it has done (and the good it has not done). Of course, there is a difference of opinion between, say, the strictness of Calvin and the humanism of Chesterton or Dostoevsky, but isn't the central idea precisely that the givenness of sin can be overcome by divine grace, should you accept it? The theological subtleties of whether salvation of the individual is predetermined need not concern us here, since they probably didn't matter for the average lay believer either, except in times of great sectarian turbulence. Still, it was not by the acts of the individual that the goal was achieved, but by one's submission to the higher authority, or, should we prefer to be cynical about it, ideological allegiance.

However, in Indian religions, for example, the starting point is radically different: eternity is what we already have, even though nothing in it is constant. The transmigrating soul of the Hindu goes through incarnation after incarnation, and there is no single divine authority to decide its fate, which is always determined by its own deeds and choices. The Buddhists take this one step further in claiming this soul is itself the illusory extension of fundamental stupidity and lust, without a nature of its own, a creation of circumstances that have themselves to be overcome. Simplifying introductions to Buddhist thought claim that it characterizes these circumstances as 'suffering'. This is not quite correct, because 'suffering' would be a condition that is opposed, within the same paradigm, to 'happiness' or some such, while for Buddhists 'happiness' and 'suffering' are at a smaller distance from each other than we would normally think. They are no more than different forms of the same basically unsatisfactory form of being to which we are condemned. For example, if we take an example of any supreme happiness or physical bliss, it is always possible precisely because of its opposition to some other state of the body or mind. Modern drugs might be able to prolong the duration of the human orgasm, for example. But what if an orgasm were to go on for a couple of hours? Two weeks? Would one rather be experiencing something else? What about six months? Would it still be physical bliss or rather a form of intolerable torture?

So the solution, from the Buddhist point of view, is not to work for and eventually 'earn' paradise, which is comparatively simple, but to get out of the works completely. Because paradise is always temporary. It is like a vacation, in the sense that it is nice while it lasts but must, and will, eventually be over. All Buddhists agree that the human condition is actually the ideal place for solving one's problems, because a human being is intelligent enough to understand what these problems are and free enough to act on that understanding, no matter how humble her/his circumstances may be. And it is not so free from care that no one can be bothered to try. Moreover, as Mahāyāna Buddhist philosophy argues, there is no salvation to be found anywhere else except in the very setting we are in: there is no *nirvāna*, no other side, no secret exit from our present condition and the only way to deal with it is to see it for what it is, without clinging to it. Simone Weil has expressed a similar view, with the structural cruelty characteristic of her thought, saying 'love of God is pure when joy and suffering inspire an *equal* degree of gratitude' (1963: 55). However, Weil is standing face to face with a transcendent absolute (which, we can suppose, gives her comfort), while the Buddhists of most denominations are almost completely on their own. Mythical or mystified figures can be helpers or guides, but they are not going to do the job instead of the human being (the Japanese 'Pure Land' variety of Buddhism is an exception).

This also means that the Buddhist tradition is not as obsessed with overcoming death as Western thought has been. Death is an aspect of existence, just as life is. So yes, death eventually comes to us all, but there are more important matters to consider.

ZB One can look from a somewhat different angle at the Buddhist solution to the formidable challenge, which the knowledge of mortality presents: how much power does it offer to mortals over their non-negotiable, inescapable immortality? Not much, it seems: not much, if measured by the Christian standard and particularly by its modern sequel.

You observe that 'the Buddhist tradition is not as obsessed with overcoming death as Western thought has been'. True indeed – but it owes that effect to the reduction of the event of death to something like a stage-station or a Post House where tired horses once used to be replaced to drive the traveller through another stretch of the road; or a momentary 'gear-change' in the otherwise continuous car trip. For the Buddhists, immortality is recycled as an endless chain of successive (corporeal, not ethereal!) reincarnations, with some causal connection between them surmised and guessed, but unknowable even in retrospect and for that reason unmanageable. Such a solution is a boon to spiritual tranquillity – there is a lot of comfort to be derived from the awareness that trajectories have been firmly, well-nigh non-negotiably, settled in advance or left to be bindingly decided in future; in both cases, however, there is little left to be done to influence, let alone determine, one's future shape. I may admire and adore the ethereal grace of the butterflies and dream to become like them – but what can I do to assure that this is what will happen in my next embodiment? I am looking for a reassuring answer – alas, in vain. What remains, as you rightly observe, is 'not to work for and eventually "earn" paradise...but to get out of the works completely'. Quietism, acceptance of things *as they come* – rather than *making* them come – is the recipe for life in this and all other incarnations.

RR Well, it is a bit more complicated than that, even though your final conclusion is quite correct. However, the main reason for this is not to be found in the essential inability of beings to control their fate, but in the impossibility of affecting it through programmatic, goal-oriented action. When we solve one problem, another is bound to arise. Of course, what a human being does affects her/his future fate in any case, just as our choices to indulge in pleasures may lead to health problems or our carelessness about the environment may affect the genetic heritage that we leave to our descendants, not to mention the world itself. Similarly, we are made up of the choices our ancestors have made, as well as our own previous ones. This is how, I think, we can interpret the idea of *karma* for the purposes of our present situation. So there is also in Buddhism a lot of sense in doing good deeds and refraining from bad ones, because both will leave their traces on the future. Another of their effects is the development of the individual's psychological inclinations. For example, in a society that prohibits everything and where even a minor expression of human weakness results in the breach of some law or other, it is almost inevitable that all but the most robotic people will find themselves on the wrong side of the law in some respect. But this, in turn, can engender nihilistic attitudes towards the law and the legitimacy of the authorities themselves. A good thing, too, because it undermines totalitarian systems more efficiently than liberal ones. However, the person who internalizes the idea that being human in her/his particular way is equivalent to being a criminal will be more likely to be persuaded to do something that would also be illegal in contexts other than her/his rather restricted circumstances. This is possibly one of the reasons why Buddhist ethics places great emphasis on thoughts of committing good and evil deeds, because they already constitute choices that will leave their mark on a person's character – or, as they put it, already generate corresponding *karma*.

On the whole, however, it is true that these systems of thought – and we might as well include Daoism here – do not promote large-scale agendas for changing the world. From my point of view, this is actually quite similar to the difference between the analytical academic and the politician who actively interferes with what happens. The two cardinal virtues of the Buddhist system are compassion and wisdom. And understanding how the world works indeed leads to the acceptance of things as they come rather than making them come, as you put it.

ZB All that you have described above is the very opposite, I'd say, of the *modern* solution – that it is all about action, a *purposeful* action aiming at control over the trajectory of fate, rendering it pliable and obedient to one's resolutions (the Buddhist 'wisdom' to which you refer is precisely the awareness that the hope for such control is futile, and that the degree of control, if any, is bound to remain untested and unknown); and that supplies the call to action with a detailed instruction on how to proceed to make that action effective. The modern solution insists that this, gaining effective control over the shape of your soul's eternal existence, is what the time-span of earthly life ought to be used for, while also reassuring you that this is something you are capable of accomplishing if only you earnestly try. Modern solution, stepping yet farther than its Christian predecessor, casts *immortality itself* as something that still needs to be earned, and a chance that may be lost.

In the modern solution, immortality is transferred from the realm of preordained fate to that of achievement: and a kind of achievement that in principle would be never final and definite – it may be strengthened or weakened, enhanced or diminished in the infinite course of time, though obviously not by its auctor who won't be then present and won't be able to add anything to her/his credentials; posthumously, after the auctor's demise, the status of her/his life achievement becomes a hostage to the fate s/he does not control – and a fate whose capricious verdicts s/he could not adumbrate with any certainty, but only guess, rightly or wrongly – as notoriously fickle future will show, changing its judgment time and again, revoking it or reasserting it. One can hedge one's bets, trying to behave in what the opinions of the time consider the best way to earn a place in the grateful memory of posterity, but no more than that. The rest – secure entrenchment in collective memory and/or in the shape of things to come, or their absence – is not what the auctors themselves can (at any rate fully) predetermine, however hard they try.

These essential features of the 'modern solution' have not been changed with the passage to 'postmodernity', 'late modernity', 'second modernity' or, indeed, 'liquid modernity' as I prefer to call our current condition. But the tactics meant to serve that modern strategy have been, and continue to be, enriched at an accelerated pace, incessantly adding contraptions and stratagems only vaguely – if at all – imagined fifteen or so years ago; most likely to be found then, if at all, in sci-fi writings. I would risk a suggestion that the centre of gravity in the on-going search for new ways of detoxifying the sting of the irritating elusiveness of immortality (as well as rendering the dream of immortality fit to be deployed in the service of economic profitability) is moving currently from the realm of entertainment (offering an 'experience of immortality', if not immortality itself, available 'on the spot', ready-made for instant consumption – and so pulling its vision down from the dreamy, unattainable heights of indefinite eternity to the category of goods-within-reach, indeed of a daily served and digested nourishment) to that of *technology*; but allow me to stress right away that, whether still in its previous habitat or shifted to the domain of technology, the idea of immortality consistently – gradually yet steadily – continues to be stripped of the aura of sanctity: it is disenchanted, thoroughly profaned and commodified. It is turning into one among uncountable objects of desire, which markets are all-too-ready to supply, and money (at any rate, big money) can buy.

One way or another, the present-day shifting of the most awesome and most indomitable of human worries to the domain of technology seems to be another case of the 'Promethean complex' and the ensuing 'Promethean envy' (the dread, anger and jealousy that overwhelm us at the sight of human-made artifacts manifesting greater skills and dexterity than we, their makers, possess or can possibly acquire) diagnosed already half a century ago by Günther Anders as one of the most menacing attributes of our technological age. And it is now the speed and precision of digital calculations that becomes the prime cause as well as the prime target of that Promethean envy. As Kevin Warwick, apparently the first human to attempt 'upgrading' of his body by grafting digital devices into his brain, and who has described the experience in great detail and flowery terms (2004), put it (or allowed his publishers to put it on the blurb of his manifesto of a book): 'Believing that machines with intelligence far beyond that of the human will eventually make the important decisions, Warwick investigates whether we can avoid obsolescence by using technology to improve on our comparatively limited capabilities.' The reasoning behind his decision to insert a computer into his body (our distant ancestors used to eat and swallow their enemies believing that such an act will transfer the power of their foes into their own bodies) we learn from Warwick's own words recorded at the very beginning of the introductory chapter: '[W]hile fate made me human, it also gave me the power to do something about it. The ability to change myself, to upgrade my human form with the aid of technology. To link my body directly with silicon; to become a cyborg – part human, part machine.'

For my lack of professional competence, I wouldn't dare prognosticate how feasible technologically the project of 'linking the body directly with silicon' will prove to be. But the minds of rising number of experts, as well as big money, are invested in rendering it feasible – so also, perhaps, plausible. In February 2011 Dmitri Itskov, a Russian oligarch, summoned the foremost sages of informatics and brain studies to join in his '2045 Initiative', whose aim, according to its English Wikipedia summary, is to design 'an artificial humanoid body (called Avatar) and an advanced brain–computer interface system. On the biological side, a life support system will be developed for hosting a human brain inside the Avatar and maintaining it alive and functional. A later phase of the project will research into the creation of an artificial brain into which the original individual consciousness may be transferred.' Itskov presented the assembled boffins with a sort of a 'road map' dividing the planned itinerary into the consecutive stages of required scientific–technical progress. By 2020, 'A robotic copy of a human body remotely capable of interpreting commands directly from the mind, and sending information back to the mind in a form that can be interpreted via brain–computer interface' will be available; by 2030, 'An Avatar with an artificial brain in which a human personality is transferred at the end of one's life'; and finally, for 2045, 'a hologram-like avatar' is planned. Let me add here that the practical attempt to transfer human mental skills to computers (a process fashioned after the pattern of manual skills already transferred all but completely to computer-operated machines) is already in full swing.

With the focus of attention drifting or being shifted to the realm of technology, another seminal, yet equally predictable, shift appears to be occurring: from the spiritual sphere to that of the corporeal. New technology drew the idea of bodily immortality, previously the exclusive reserve of the Second Coming prophets and science-fiction writers, into the universe of the practical and the realistic. Genetic engineering, bionics, the technology of cyborgization and, last but not least, cloning, all promise immortality of the body – or, at any rate, infinitely extendable duration of its 'usability'. In his *Possibility of an Island* (2005), perhaps the most powerful, elaborate and indeed realistic-sounding – and so also frightening – of dystopias since Zamiatin, Orwell or Huxley, Michel Houellebecq connected the prospect of transferring human personality, complete with its memory, with the already developing technology of cloning – to adumbrate the updated and technologically feasible form in which eternity of personal life may be attained: and to paint, in lurid colours, the social and psychical consequences of that attainment for the neo-humans.

Not being an expert on either of the above-listed technologies, and obliged therefore to rely on the opinions of specialists notorious for their controversies, I am evidently unfit to adjudicate on whether, and how much, that promise is warranted. I can only note the impact that the very presence of such promise, rendered yet more trustworthy courtesy of the scoop-hungry media, is already making on the shape of the popular fear/awe of, and the lust for, immortality, and the direction in which it tends to be channelled – or the conduits through which the resulting concerns and apprehensions tend to be unloaded.

Having said all that about the most recent departures in the un-ended, and in all probability unending, story of the mortals' romance with immortality, allow me all the same to retreat, for a moment, four and a half millennia, to the 'Epic of Gilgamesh': 'Fill your belly with good things; day and night, night and day, dance and be merry, feast and rejoice. Let your clothes be fresh, bathe yourself in water, cherish the little child that holds your hand, and make your wife happy in your embrace' – thus spake Siduri, the woman maker of wine, to Gilgamesh, having reminded him first that his expedition to the land of immortality is doomed, because 'when gods created man they allotted to him death'. But in a stark opposition to Siduri's advice, this was Gilgamesh's answer to his bosom friend and companion Enkidu's complaint that 'the cry of sorrow sticks in my throat, I am oppressed by idleness': 'I will go to the country where the cedar is felled. I will set up my name in the place where the names of famous men are written, and where no man's name is written I will raise a monument to the gods. Because of the evil that is in the land, we will go to the forest and destroy the evil.'

These were, I believe, the first two recorded human responses to the discovery of their human – all-too-human – foredoomed mortality (recorded, let's note, still in cuneiform: a thousand and a half years before the *Iliad*). A third response – has it been found since? The jury (if there is a jury!) is still most certainly out.

And allow me one last addition – a quotation from Todd May's book *Death* (2009), brought recently to my attention by my daughter Anna Sfard. Death, the author of the book suggests, is 'a disease whose cure, if it existed, would be worse than the disease itself'. Wholeheartedly, I agree. And this is how Todd May himself explained the sense of his suggestion in an interview given to Matt Bieber: 'trajectory [of life] is a limited one and therefore it matters what that trajectory has looked like and what it's going to look like' (2013). In other words, without mortality, life would have no meaning. It is thanks to the awareness of mortality, a 'lived through' mortality, that it has. As, a few decades before Todd May, the great ethical philosopher Hans Jonas insisted, it is thanks to our awareness of our mortality that the days count and we count them. This is the truth that Jorge Luis Borges, in his immortal story of 'The Immortal', narrated so beautifully, and so convincingly, leaving no room for doubt. A truth which the animals, were they able to compose narratives and write them down, would most certainly endorse. But they don't compose narratives; neither could they compose them if they wished – but they can't wish. And no wonder. After all, for all they know, as long as they stay alive, they are immortal.

RR   Yes. And it is not just a utopian project of an ambitious businessman craving immortality. If we are to believe Stephen Hawking, this old idea proclaimed by science fiction for decades is now approaching reality, as have so many others: even though the current stage of science does not allow for it yet, it is quite possible that at a certain moment a technology will be developed that enables its owners to upload the human brain into cyber-space. 'I think the brain is like a programme in the mind, which is like a computer, so it's theoretically possible to copy the brain onto a computer and so provide a form of life after death', he says (Collins 2013). In other words, if there are any parts of the brain that do not work like computer software, they do not matter and can be discarded. This is precisely where I have to part company with the techno-optimists. Even if I cannot prove this scientifically, I do not believe that human language (in the broadest sense of the word, including all ways of notation, formulaic representation and so on) will ever be able to describe reality exhaustively. So there is always something that remains beyond our reach. We can make almost true copies of everything, but almost true copies are what they are – *almost* true. Machines, it seems, are already able to 3D-print working organs of living bodies, but I refuse to believe that they are – how should I put it? – structurally selfsame with organs that have actually grown within such organisms. Which is not to say that this isn't a wonderful development in technology that can prolong the lives and relieve the suffering of many people – just as previous technological aids to our health and being have. In that sense, is the entrance of computers into our organisms in fact so fundamentally different from that of wooden legs, glasses and pacemakers? Is it because computers can calculate that they are more alien than this other stuff? Or is it because the targeted consumer of contemporary biotechnology is somebody who does not have a health problem to begin with – someone who wants to enhance and change the human condition to a technologically upgraded one beyond our present capabilities?

ZB I share your premonitions and apprehensions. You fear, as I do, that some crucial human powers might suffer in the result of their transference to computers meant – and believed by many – to expand and enhance them. I wish to add but one more reason to fear the expropriation of human mental capacities by computers.

Human creative powers can be traced to precisely those inadequacies of human language which computer designers intended, and computers are seen by many as promising, to eliminate. Edmund Leach, one of the most inquisitive anthropologists of the past century, heavily influenced by Claude Lévi-Strauss' structuralist programme and practices (see, e.g., Leach 1964 and 1966), traced the notorious restlessness of human culture and of human potential, as well as the human inborn inclination and impulse to transcendence, back to the endemic – and, in his view, ineradicable – shortcoming of language (any 'natural' language): to its innate and connate incapacity to reach the ideal of precision identified as *Eindeutigkeit* – its own ambition and/or pretension to 're-present' reality *unambiguously*.

The shortcoming in question is, according to Leach, the insuperable discrepancy between the inherent *discreteness* of the words' semantic fields (indispensable for the fulfilment of the communicative function of language) and the seamless *continuity* of reality. The inevitable and incurable outcomes of that discrepancy are twofold. On the one hand, unnamed (and so unnoticed and unrecorded) 'blank spots' are left between the 'named' semantic fields of experience; it is for that reason that reality, as you rightly indicate, would never be 'exhaustively described'. On the other, some semantic fields overlap partly or marginally, and so generate spaces of experience overloaded with meanings – all too often contradictory and irreconcilable meanings.

The first outcome awakes the exploratory spirit in human subjects – prone as we are to wander beyond the realm of the routine and the familiar into novel, strange and poorly mapped territories. The search for a fixed set of connections between stimuli and responses, perceptions and patterns of conduct, which we badly need in order to proceed with confidence and to steer clear of erroneous moves, is doomed to remain forever anything but complete: the history of knowledge (including its future history) can be retold as a story of explorations and discoveries, of naming and filling the successive 'blank spots' on the map of the *Lebenswelt*. The second outcome however is the obtrusive and irritating presence inside that *Lebenswelt* of spaces burdened with an excess of meanings: overloaded with mutually inconsistent senses, evoking/stimulating contradictory action patterns and defying a straightforward, let alone obvious and self-evident choice between them. In short, it is the creation of areas of confused and confusing perceptions, rendering an effective action difficult or downright impossible: expanses of ambivalence, disorientation and discomfiture.

Let me quote, please, from my old study of *Modernity and Ambivalence*:

> Ambivalence, the possibility of assigning an object or an event to more than one category, is a language-specific disorder: a failure of the naming (segregating) function that language is meant to perform. The main symptom of disorder is the acute discomfort we feel when we are unable to read the situation properly and to choose between alternative actions... Ambivalence is a side product of the labour of classification; and it calls for yet more classifying effort. (1991: 1–3)

Those new and improved classifying efforts, forever renewed in the hope for a greater transparency of the world and for one's own capacity to act in it and on it, are the engines of cultural history; they are particularly intense in the modern era. Above all, they are now conscious and cast at the centre of attention – made into objects of systematic, continuous and assiduous care.

We may say that existence is modern in as far as it is saturated by a 'without us, a deluge' feeling. And that means: in as far as war is declared on all and any ambivalence and on the areas particularly prone to generate it and particularly resistant to 'ordering', and in as far as such 'between and betwixt' areas overloaded with divergent and discordant meanings are (to use Leach's suggestion) tabooed: suppressed – or, if possible, eliminated. The labour of making humans feel comfortable and *chez soi* in the world declared by the modern spirit to be a *human* task. Human – all too human. And *only* human.

2

Selves in Language

Rein Raud   The relation of selfhood to language is indeed crucial. I'd say there are actually even two separate ranges of topics here, which we could preliminarily distinguish as 'internal' and 'external', even though the individual may not always be conscious of that difference. The 'internal' repertoire of linguistic tools that we use to make sense of the world, both in silence and in communicating with others, should not be mixed up with how the ways we speak make us 'externally' appear to those we speak to. Of course they are sides of the same coin, yet I think the processes of self-conceptualization and self-presentation, both intentional and spontaneous, still appear as relatively independent from each other and are affected by multitudes of other factors. So I guess it is reasonable to tackle them one by one.

You are most certainly right about the limits of language. I'm not even quite certain whether it is at all plausible to speak about completely overlapping semantic fields shared by different people and/or in different situations. As cognitive anthropologists and some linguists have suggested, we do not really operate with concepts, but with 'schemas' or 'frames', that is, constructions that allow every user of the corresponding word to fill in some blanks or to highlight some nuances in her/his mind. Words like 'house', 'dog' or 'grandpa' evoke quite different images for each person who uses them. Moreover, Dan Sperber and Deirdre Wilson have argued rather persuasively (1998) that when two people talk to each other, each only understands maybe 70 per cent of what the other one says. Not surprisingly, however, this is quite enough for successful communication – because we have learned to live with it. Similarly, Yuri Lotman, one of the founders of cultural semiotics, has shown that 'the functionality of a highly complex sign system does not at all presuppose full comprehension, but a state of tension between comprehension and non-comprehension' (1992: 99). Lotman is more concerned with artistic use of language, but the same principle applies anywhere. However, this is not necessarily only a negative thing. The ambivalence that you have so aptly diagnosed can also be seen as the site where our selves come into being, at every moment when they come into contact with their world and have to make a choice about how they understand it. Overcoming ambivalence – for our own, 'internal' purposes, that is – can be seen as a form of self-realization, an activity that makes the world we inhabit more fully our own, even though we can never overcome this ambivalence completely. Nor should we. The ambivalence of the world is a challenge that keeps us alive. Of course, not all of what keeps us alive is always pleasant, desirable or even easy to come to terms with, but nonetheless the alternative – to be without it – would bring about the loss of who we *are*.

So if there is a strict meaning to be found anywhere at all, perhaps we should look for it among the kind of words that refer to impersonal concepts, definable ideas we do not directly experience, for example scientific formulae or legal terms. But the latter, at least, are intensely debated at every step precisely because any particular, real conflict of interests requires their application to the personal experiences of human beings who interpret them in their different selfish ways. But this just happens to be the way we look at everything. Thus, in a sense, each of us lives in a narrative of predominantly our own writing.

Now this seems to imply a tiny contradiction. On the one hand, we exist in part through overcoming the ambivalence of the world – reaching out for it, as it were; on the other hand, however, we are bound to integrate everything we touch in a web of our own making – the 'web of meanings' of Weber and Vygotsky. We are observing darkness with a lamp in our hands, so to speak. What I would like to suggest, however, is that the way of looking at language that presupposes transparency and adequacy is itself faulted, even though it looks very logical or even natural. In its pure form, this standpoint only emerged as a modern phenomenon, not surprisingly in the work of Descartes, who wrote, in a letter to Mersenne, on 20 November 1629:

> If someone were to explain correctly what are the simple ideas in the human imagination out of which all human thoughts are compounded, and if his explanation were generally received, I would dare hope for a universal language very easy to learn, to speak and to write. The greatest advantage of such a language would be the assistance it would give to men's judgment, representing matters so clearly that it would be almost impossible to go wrong. (1991: 13)

This universal language would indeed be wholly transparent, and, if it were possible, then natural languages would start to look like deviations from this synthetic ideal. The issue is precisely that this kind of language is impossible in principle, at least for anyone sharing the human condition. First of all, because the possibility of making mistakes is a *sine qua non* of being human, or being alive in general. How else could something new come into being? And second, because a unified and standardized system of simple ideas precludes individuality, or reduces it to the level of combination of elements from a limited, unchangeable set. Obviously such combinations are necessarily finite in number. But it is certainly understandable how this kind of thinking can lead to fantasies about uploadable human brains.

Zygmunt Bauman *Eindeutigkeit* – un-ambiguity – of language is and remains, I repeat, the lodestar of the modern spirit. That star leads its carriers from one astonishing breakthrough to another, but not an inch closer either to the 'theory of everything' to which it is believed by the cutting-edge physics of the day to point, or to the site where that 'universal language very easy to learn, to speak and to write' was hoped by Descartes to be found. But can the infuriating lack of fit between words and things, language and reality, be cured by reform of language? In a paper called symptomatically 'Physics's Pangolin', Margaret Wertheim has written:

Theoretical physics is beset by a paradox that remains as mysterious today as it was a century ago: at the subatomic level things are simultaneously particles and waves. Like the duck-rabbit illusion first described in 1899 by the Polish-born American psychologist Joseph Jastrow, subatomic reality appears to us as two different categories of being.

But there is another paradox in play. Physics itself is riven by the competing frameworks of quantum theory and general relativity, whose differing descriptions of our world eerily mirror the wave–particle tension. When it comes to the very big and the extremely small, physical reality appears to be not one thing, but two. Where quantum theory describes the subatomic realm as a domain of individual quanta, all jitterbug and jumps, general relativity depicts happenings on the cosmological scale as a stately waltz of smooth flowing space-time. General relativity is like Strauss – deep, dignified and graceful. Quantum theory, like jazz, is disconnected, syncopated, and dazzlingly modern.

On the one hand, then, physics is taken to be a march toward an ultimate understanding of reality; on the other, it is seen as no different in status to the understandings handed down to us by myth, religion and, no less, literary studies. Because I spend my time about equally in the realms of the sciences and arts, I encounter a lot of this dualism. Depending on whom I am with, I find myself engaging in two entirely different kinds of conversation. Can we all be talking about the same subject?

And she concludes, referring to Mary Douglas, a formidable structural anthropologist:

To put this into Douglas's terms, the powers that have been attributed to physicists' structure of ideas have been overreaching. 'Attempts to force experience into logical categories of non-contradiction' have, she would say, inevitably failed. From the contemplation of wave–particle pangolins we have been led to the limits of the linguistic system of physicists…Will we accept, at some point, that there are limits to the quantification project, just as there are to all taxonomic schemes? Or will we be drawn into ever more complex and expensive quests – CERN mark two, Hubble, the sequel – as we try to root out every lingering paradox? In Douglas's view, ambiguity is an inherent feature of language that we must face up to, at some point, or drive ourselves into distraction. (2013)

And so, as we see, our failure (or more exactly the failure of the philosophers ruminating on the imperfections of human understanding) to follow the lodestar to where it was supposed to lead can't be explained by methodological blunders or scientific immaturity. We are not the only hunters on a wild goose chase. There is, I suppose, something that unites the plight of the most sophisticated languages parading an unimpeachable stamp of scientific authority with the status of 'understandings handed down to us by myth, religion and, no less, literary studies'. And this something is the essential un-commensurability of the two functions cojoint in language: the communicative and the representational.

It is because of that insuperable out-of-jointness of the two synchronic functions that Lotman's 'state of tension between comprehension and non-comprehension' is to stay – here and there and everywhere...To perform the communicative functions, representation needs to resign its ambition of, and its pretension to, exhaustiveness and *Eindeutigkeit*. Acting on that ambition and claiming that pretension would in turn sap the communicative efficiency of locutions. And there is a sound reason to suspect that the latter consequence is indeed a latent, even if not manifest, function of the esoteric jargon of the humanities, chronically unsure as they are of their scientific status and so eager to earn scientific credentials through the emulation of the natural-scientific incomprehensibility to a lay reader/listener.

RR Perhaps the problem of ambiguity has even deeper roots and is derived from our understanding of how representation works. The majority of Western thinkers from Aristotle to the present, collectively agreeing perhaps on little else, seem to share the view that reality itself has some kind of a logical structure, which natural languages reflect to the best of their abilities, even if imperfectly. However, when we look around, we see that outside the West this belief is rather rarely to be found. Indeed, it is much easier to think of language as an order in its own right, not an imitation of reality, but something superimposed on it. The structural variability of the languages of the world is so immense and they have so few elements in common that it is simply impossible to reduce them all to some kind of identical set of deep structures, the efforts of Steven Pinker and his associates notwithstanding.

This does not mean that I would endorse a strong version of the Sapir–Whorf hypothesis either. Language does not necessarily pre-determine the total scope of what an individual can perceive in the world, but that does not mean that it has no effect on it either. This has been proven experimentally: Paul Kay and Willet Kempton gave the same task to two groups of people, speakers of English and Tarahumara, which does not distinguish between blue and green. They had to divide three kinds of chips (blue, dark green and light green) into just two categories according to their colour. The dark green chips were actually physically closer to blue, and this is precisely how Tarahumara speakers perceived them, yet speakers of English grouped them with light green, with which they shared their linguistic characteristic (Kay and Kempton 1984). This is by far not the only type of interference language causes in the perception process, but it should suffice to show that the imperfections of our language are inevitably carried over into the way we perceive our world, in many ways and at every moment.

However, the essential incommensurability that you pointed out between communication and representation inevitably takes this even further. Our view of the world is incomplete from the start, and still we try to eliminate the ambiguity that has leaked through the linguistic filters to make it yet more faulty. Perhaps this is caused by a wish to foreclose interiority, or 'subjectivity' in the sense of individual bias, in favour of 'objectivity', or a shared bias. But even a brief look at how the process of communication works should show us that interiority is not to be dispensed with. The communication schemes of Claude Shannon and Roman Jakobson leave the impression that the operation of 'decoding' is merely a mirror process of 'coding' – that the same movements occur, only in an opposite order. This is quite clearly not so. When we code, we look in our mental dictionaries for appropriate signs to repre-sent the ideas, or conceptual structures, we want to share with others. Most usually we have a certain choice, and we opt for the least inadequate, because no word can express absolutely every-thing that an individual mind compresses into an elementary idea. When we decode, we have to turn these signs back into conceptual structures again. But we only have the singular signs that made it into the message, and are not privy to the deliberations that made the speaker prefer one of these signs to all others. And since natural language is never as strict as, for example, the Morse code, which establishes a correspondence between certain signals and letters, it is impossible to translate the message back into the very same ideas that produced it. Because there simply is no finite repository of elementary ideas that we all share.

I am sorry for going on for such a long time about something quite elementary, but I think it is very relevant to what you and Wertheim have to say about the language of science. An important element of the move by which scientific authority establishes itself is precisely this denial of interiority – of our own immediate contact with the world in which we live: in other words, physicalism, the thesis that everything can be described by physics, an assumption most natural scientists tend to share to a certain degree. I have no problem with a weak version of physicalism, a view that everything that happens in reality can *also* be described in terms of physics, but somehow, almost unnoticeably, quite a few of its proponents have shifted to the much stronger position that such physical description is also the most exhaustive and most adequate one. Such a view entails a redefinition of reality, because it simply refuses to see anything for which a physical explanation is not the most informative – for example, any occurrence of meaning. From the physicalist point of view, meanings are not quite real. From my point of view, however, explaining speech by a precise description of undulations of air produced by the human articulatory apparatus does not get us very far.

Or let us take a look at the most abstract of cultural languages, music, which is also universal. Even though music can be notated and then reproduced from notes, it carries the minimum of informational content. The effect of music cannot be reduced to the relation between the notes and the sound-types they represent. Moreover, the same notes can produce quite different effect when played by a virtuoso and a beginner, even if formally the music may be the same. A physicalist description of the differences between these two performances is possible, but insufficient for explaining why in one case the audience may welcome it with standing ovations, and in the other, with merely polite encouragement. What I want to say is that there is such 'music' in every act of using a language, not in the euphony of sounds, not in the intonations, but in the part that cannot be adequately transcribed by any means of notation.

So perhaps, if we want to bring an element of interiority into our view of language, we should talk not only about communication, but also about co-experiencing, following late Wittgenstein. A linguistic act is successful not when the maximum amount of information gets across, but when the experiences of its participants are closest to each other, if only for a moment. I may come to the same internal conclusions, drawing upon the resources of my own life experience, or acquired knowledge, to understand the position from which the utterance has been made. Of course, I may then totally disagree with it, but I have co-experienced what has been said. I have heard that some film directors let control viewers see their films without the sound at first, thinking their work a success only if what happens can be understood without the words as well.

ZB In the action of communicating, 'interiority' is a kind of obstacle that can't be engaged in a battle and kicked out of the way; it can be only passed around in silence or – better still – denied or left out of sight! To serve the task of communication, language we use needs to abstain from the doomed intention to engage with the inaccessible. And what is inaccessible is precisely what you locate in the 'interiority'. When I ask you to hand me a green pen, I can count on you meeting my request even if I have no idea – and never will have – what sort of impression the sound signal 'green' evokes in your 'interiority'. Is what you see identical, or totally dissimilar from what I see in my 'interiority' when hearing that call? Well, this is an absurd question, akin to asking what it is like at 5pm on the Sun. Thanks to God or Nature, the shrewdness and dexterity of language renders questions of such sort totally irrelevant to the success of communication (as Ludwig Wittgenstein famously and soberingly reminded us, 'to understand' means to know how to go on).

All those stratagems and contraptions described by Leach[1] are neither blunders yelling for rectification, nor leftovers of bygone mistakes now waiting for a cleaning operation, but *sine-qua-non* conditions of the language's proficiency and efficiency in acquitting itself of the task of communicating. Take for instance the notorious (and at first sight extravagantly wasteful) redundancy

---

[1] See, for instance, Leach (1964) and (1971).

in both spelling and syntax: a closer look reveals, however, that, far from being a useless and unnecessary, uncalled-for complexity and burden, it is a welcome contrivance – radically diminishing the chance of mistaken reading of the message even if the sender was not pedantic enough when correcting spelling and syntactic errors in her or his writing performance. In pursuit of communicative fitness, languages hedge – need to hedge – their bets.

And so what seem to be flaws and drawbacks to complain about are in fact ingenious solutions deserving of admiration. We need to study them, be aware of them – and to live with them for the duration. The clash and tussle between the tasks of communication and the motives inspiring and guiding the effort of representation are here to stay. And I countersign with both my hands your assertion that 'explaining speech by a precise description of undulations of air produced by the human articulatory apparatus does not get us very far'. I would even, instead of the circumspect and rather lenient 'does not get us very far', put bluntly that it 'leads us too far on the road to nowhere'.

RR Precisely. Suppose I am colour-blind and ashamed to talk about it. Your request to hand you the green pen will push me into a desperate helplessness. Or maybe I am bitter about my deficiency, and consider any reference to it as a deliberate attempt to humiliate me. If you now tell me none of this was your intent, you will be referring to your own interiority, but in this context that should not be available as a counter-argument. Any simple request thus has to balance itself carefully on the scale between rudeness and courtesy, to be neither so rude that it would be resented, nor so polite as to sound ironical. So even the request to hand you the green pen has to rely on a plane of co-experiencing in order to be effective. And this is something that cannot be adequately defined in rational and neutral terms. Consider the failure of mechanical political correctness: listing certain words as offensive and replacing them with more suitable substitutes never solves the problem, because the same derogatory attitudes get so easily transferred to the new expressions that these start to sound politically just as incorrect in no time.

So there is no way to look at language carefully without taking interiority into account. What I wanted to say is that there is no such strict opposition or border between interiority and the outside that we could put our finger on. There is a shared aspect or dimension to our interiorities, one that cannot be adequately described in physicalist terms, and this shared aspect is at work always when we use language.

However, all of this is not to say that co-experience necessarily creates a context of shared values or ideas. On the contrary, it can be the site of irreconcilable clashes. Perhaps a better way to describe the situation is as one of opening up our communication channels, and experiencing both our own limitations and those of our partner in the exchange at the same time. So, it may be only momentarily, but something like the 'fusion of horizons' described by Hans-Georg Gadamer (2004: 305) is taking place. This is something that makes us more vulnerable for a moment to something unexpected, coming from the outside, also forcing us to question our own being here and now. It does not have to be dramatic to be real. And it does not have to be provocative. Sometimes unquestioning conformity to norms can be as unsettling – for example, when a Westerner sees a Muslim woman at a loss when she is offered the possibility of breaking with the behavioural stereotypes we, as outsiders, think are imposed on her against her own will. Or when an intelligent soldier complies with obviously stupid orders coming down from above. I cannot even begin to understand anything someone else wants to tell me without conjuring up, within my interiority, a preliminary and inescapably incorrect picture of who that someone is.

ZB What you are speaking of in that allegory of a colour-blind man asked to hand over the green pen leads us from the murky universe of monadic interiorities to the bony and fleshy encounter between them leading (or not) to a dialogue...Martin Buber had set apart the case of *Begegnung* (meeting, genuine) and *Vergegnung* (failed meeting, 'mismeeting'). As a sociologist first, and a philosopher as a remote second, I am interested primarily in *social settings* (rather than trying to fathom the essentially recondite, impenetrable/inscrutable as we've already agreed, depth of the 'interiority'); the settings that enhance the likelihood of one rather than another of the alternative possibilities occurring. And the alternatives, as the *NYT* columnist Charles M. Blow spelled them out when writing about the deepening divisiveness of the

American political debate, are – as in all and any case of choosing
between them – the following:

> For better or worse, ours is a two-party system, and I fervently
> believe that a healthy, idea-oriented opposition helps keep everyone
> honest. If we disagree on the size and role of government, let's have
> that debate. If we disagree on the role America should play in
> helping to police the world's quarrels, let's have that debate. If we
> disagree on the best way to jump start the economy, best prepare
> our children, fix our broken immigration system or adjust our
> system of taxation, let's have all those debates. But when the debate
> devolves into invectives born of hate – racist, misogynistic, homo-
> phobic or otherwise – it ceases to be healthy or productive and
> instead dredges up the worst of who we were and, in some cases,
> remain. (2014a)

Speaking about the debate devolving 'into invectives born of hate',
Blow singled out, as particularly odious among recent examples,
a certain Ted Nugent, who described Barack Obama, the current
American President, as a 'communist-raised, communist-educated,
communist-nurtured subhuman mongrel'. 'Subhuman', as he
points out, was drawn from the Nazi description of Jews. 'Mongrel'
can be traced to a similarly racist Nazi progeny (*Mischling*), but
also to the colonial derogatory term 'half-caste' – though it has
been by now fully assimilated and absorbed by the anti-black
jingoist vocabulary. This being the US with its firmly settled and
fixed horrors of 'reds under the bed', the qualifier 'communist'
played in Nugent's harangue just the role of a dot over an 'i' and
the crossing of a 't' in declaring a person so described unfit for
the role of a conversation partner and relegating him or her off-
limits in the debate. 'Invectives born of hate' appear in speech in
the role of (to use Bronisław Malinowski's term) 'phatic expressions', or (to use John Austin's terminology) 'perlocutions'. The
information they convey is an intention/resolution of the speaker
to prevent the eventual encounter from turning into a genuine
meeting; of *refusal* to enter a dialogue and switching the responsibility for the refusal to the other's lack of fitness and suitability
for the status of conversing subject.

Pope Francis offered recently an example of conduct representing exactly the opposite of the strategy of Nugent and his ilk. The
very first interview of his pontificate was with Eugenio Scalfari,

who presents himself in public as a 'catholic-bred atheist', to be printed in the Italian daily *La Repubblica*, known to hold a consistently anticlerical stance. The message conveyed by that gesture could not be clearer: dialogue is the proper response to the extant diversification of humanity and the desirable mode of human interdependence and cohabitation, and dialogue means conversing with people holding to opinions and convictions *different* from your own; conversation narrowed to people sharing your own beliefs is not a genuine dialogue. And the purpose of a dialogue is not a defeat of those thinking differently, but mutual understanding and joint effort to elaborate the mutually beneficial *modus vivendi* with a difference. It was as if Pope Francis was following Richard Sennett's prescription for dialogue to be informal, open and cooperative: 'informal', as started without *a priori* fixed procedural rules but allowing such rules to emerge and be tested in the course of the dialogue; 'open', as the participants enter it ready to allow for the eventuality of being proved wrong and prepared to correct their initially held convictions; and 'cooperative', as the aim of the dialogue is not the split of the participants into winners and losers, but enrichment of the experience, understanding and knowledge of them all.

The big issue which I believe to be of utmost importance in the present-day under-defined and under-determined coexistence of interdependent selves of variegated identities is the social conditions that favour entering dialogue vs their opposites – social settings that prompt avoiding it. At the moment, the second type seems to be prevailing. We witness dialogues falling apart and grinding to a halt much more often than being earnestly initiated and seen through. The temptation to resort to the construction of *sui generis* 'echo chambers' (exchanges in which the only sounds one hears are echoes of one's own voice) or 'halls of mirrors' (in which the only sights one sees are reflections of one's face) appear to be ever more common.

RR This brings us to another, although closely related, set of problems: the 'external' side of our linguistic selves, or the ways in which the language we use makes us appear to others. There is an insurmountable gap between the internality of our language, or the place where the meaningful world is happening for us, and the verbal outside of our being, which primarily takes place under conditions not of our own making. Everything we do is somehow affected by this disjunction. When I reach out my hand to take the penultimate piece of cake from the plate, this action, as well as the intent behind it, is seen differently by myself and by others. But speaking is special, for at least three reasons. First of all, speaking is our primary manner of self-expression, enabling us to cover the greatest range of semantic meaning as well as nuances of modality with the greatest precision available to us (which mercifully still is not as precise as natural sciences would want to have it); second, because, unlike violin-playing or figure-skating, speech as a way of self-expression is shared by almost everybody, and finally, because speech and to a certain extent even its nuances can be notated and described in meta-languages that are also detailed enough for the purposes of the describer and mostly not too complicated to master. I can explain to a child what irony is, or how politeness works, without reverting to specialist linguistic terms – but if I did that, I could cover even more ground, almost as much as there is to cover. This is also why the friendship of Roman Jakobson, the systematic linguist, and Claude Lévi-Strauss, the rebel anthropologist, proved to be so fruitful and influential: the structures of language provide the most applicable model for all the meaning-making activities that human culture consists of – the conceptualization of social structures included. And so we hear Roland Barthes speaking about 'vestemes', or minimal meaning-carrying units in the language of clothing, which help us to explain why certain dress is required on certain occasions or what people can express about themselves by choosing a certain style of clothing when they have a choice between several (1990).

This latter situation is actually where the 'linguistic externality' of our selves comes into play. On the one hand, we have to be aware of how what we say is going to be interpreted by others, and try to be careful not to say anything we did not intend; and on the other hand, we can consciously navigate the fairly wide range of choice between ways of self-expression in most circumstances. Or perhaps the range is illusory more often than we think, and the choice to use it a breach of some unwritten rules. Because otherwise it would be difficult to explain why most people choose to emulate a model of speech rather than to create their own. So we hear long and solemn speeches at festive events that neither the speaker wants to pronounce nor the listeners to hear, and almost identical small talk repeated by different people on different occasions, when in conversation with friendly semi-strangers.

It seems to me that this is also one of the biggest impediments to dialogue in the sense that you have defined it. Most of the time, people do not speak from within their interiority, but from a pre-defined speaker-position that they have decided to adopt, be it one of a punk-rocker, a priest, a salesperson, a left-wing intellectual, a politician, a therapist or a stand-up comedian. Because this makes further conversation so much easier. Of course, from the point of view of fostering social process, a dialogue between speaker-positions can be just as meaningful, as shown by the one between a priest and a left-wing intellectual you brought up as an example. By this act of dialogue, the Pope actually managed to alter the speaker-position into which his calling had led him, and this is admirable. Yet I'm afraid a pope can still only move within a fairly circumscribed circle of choices, because if he were to act quite unpredictably, he would lose his credibility as being what he is and has to stand for. I've seen a deplorably large number of people in my life who have been elected to some office or other because they had in themselves the promise of changing things – and who have rather quickly started to speak and act as the system expects them to, that very system they had set out to alter. This is the way systems work: they do not respond to your actions if you do not adopt the correct position from within which to act, and if you do, you are no longer able to act.

But this now raises an interesting problem. From my point of view, adopting a speaker-position that has been imposed on you – especially when this is done uncritically – is an act of violence against yourself. This is the precondition of being successfully oppressed. This is what Gayatri Spivak was challenging in her seminal article entitled 'Can the Subaltern Speak?' (1988). Thus, supposedly, what we should do is to get rid of, or at least to con-sciously try to neutralize, the external matrix imposed on our speech at any given moment. Because, otherwise, a genuine meeting of minds in Buber's sense would hardly be possible, we would be repeating to each other the pleasing, but unproductive, words of pre-existing scripts from a conversation guide. But what if the availability and enforcement of such scripts have a deeper reason? Perhaps they exist because otherwise there would be too many

Ted Nugents running around and speaking their unqualified mind, filling our public space with hatred and turning insults into a norm? After all, the Pope also chose a well-educated intellectual for having a dialogue with, and not a stone-throwing militant. And yet, aren't these militants also a product of Enlightenment and its structural promise of emancipation for everyone?

ZB You put tremendously heavy emphasis on the 'insurmountable gap between the internality of our language, or the place where the meaningful world is happening for us, and the verbal outside of our being, which primarily takes place under conditions not of our own making'. The gap, you suggest in so many words but also even more strongly between the lines, derives from the pressure of external circumstances on how we form – render communicative – our reports of the state, standpoints and axiological preferences of our inner selves. In other words, externality in which verbal communication takes place is a slushy ground on which we wouldn't be able to move safely and reach the intended destination without the assistance of ready-made and ready-to-use walking implements. I agree fully with all that; where my doubts arise, however, is your apparent selection of the above-described 'fact of the matter' (that is, the necessity of facing up to the inflexible externality and compromising with its 'musts') as the paramount, perhaps even the only, constraint imposed on the 'meeting of selves'. This would be the case, were we in full awareness of the contents and standpoint of our 'interior', and so in full knowledge of what our selves would say were they not facing that externally set quandary. In other words: were there a true, self-contained 'self' prevented by external pressures from speaking up honestly, truly and freely. These conditions, however, are, I suppose, hardly ever met.

Such an idea of an 'authentic self' that precedes all attempts to articulate it discursively is a modern invention; and a derivative, I believe, of another, yet more fundamental modern innovation – the idea of 'nation' as 'naturally set apart', self-enclosed, and inhabiting a compact as well as rightfully sovereign territory (a departure that can in my view also be described as a passage from the formula 'cuius regio eius religio', proclaimed in the 1555 Westphalian settlement to replacing it, for all practical intents and purposes, by one of 'cuius regio eius natio' 300 years later, in and around the 1848 'Spring of Nations'). The vision of the 'authentic self' as a natural and therefore pre-defined and pre-determined, pre-discursive phenomenon preceding (and flouting in advance) all attempts at its expression and articulation, a cultural and psychological entity immune to all external intervention and staunchly resistant to external pressures from laws and policies – was indispensable to sustaining the political formula of the independent and sovereign nation in an independent and sovereign state. A collateral effect of that fateful departure was, in Richard Sennett's words, the nineteenth-century nationalism entrenching 'what we may call the modern ground-rule for having an identity. You have the strongest identity when you aren't aware you "have" it; you just *are* it. That is, you are most yourself when you are least aware of yourself' (2011: 61).

I suggest, however, that we take a closer look at what Fernando Pessoa noted – though in his inimitable and uncompromisingly impressionistic, poetic idiom – in *The Book of Disquiet* (1991). Let me start from the most poignant observations that cast the neat separation of 'interior' and 'exterior' into serious, indeed fundamental, doubt:

> Each of us is more than one person, many people, a proliferation of our one self... In the vast colony of our being there are different kinds of people, all thinking and feeling differently. (1991: 14).

> Everything that surrounds us becomes part of us, it seeps into us with every experience of the flesh and of life and, like the web of the great Spider, binds us subtly to what is near, ensnares us in a fragile cradle of slow death, where we lie rocking in the wind. Everything is us and we are everything. (1991: 11)

What follows from this is anything but a clear, transparent, structured whole amenable to dissection and reassembly, or for that matter to a complete inventory and rational reconstruction: 'My soul is a hidden orchestra. I know not what instruments, what fiddlestrings and harps, drums and tambours I sound and clash inside myself. All I hear is the symphony' (1991: 8). Finally:

> My soul is a black maelstrom, a great madness spinning about a vacuum, the swirling of a vast ocean around a hole in the void, and in the waters, more like whirlwinds than waters, float images

of all I ever saw or heard in the world: houses, faces, books, boxes, snatches of music and fragments of voices, all caught up in a sinister, bottomless whirlpool.

And I, I myself, am the centre that exists only because the geometry of the abyss demands it; I am the nothing around which all that spins, I exist so that it can spin, I am a centre that exists only because every circle has one. (1991: 9)

To put it bluntly: that 'centre' called '*my* self' is a postulate of Reason seeking logic in the illogical and order in chaos; 'self' is, as Pessoa suggests, a geometric fiction, a Reason-begotten construct to serve the retelling of the madness that can't be intelligibly told as an intelligible story. We draw borderlines, cut the un-embraceable wholes into manageable fragments, compose such bits in sequences and designs – but will all that bustle and mental flurry bring us any closer to the truth of that maelstrom and whirlwind? Or would it rather cover up that truth?

I suppose that at the bottom of our confusion lies the fact (if you allow me to resort once more to the same trope) that we – each one of us, complete with a body and a soul – are violins, but also the violinists who play them, and the listeners expected to be competent and are nudged to claim competence to judge the quality of sounds. Must I add that we are not soloists, but members of a symphonic orchestra that most of the time performs without a score and with no conductor, and which we call 'society'? To add yet more fog to the picture, as if the mist thus far was not dense enough, 'the idea that other people are like us and must therefore feel like us' Pessoa calls 'the central error of the literary imagination'. And he adds: 'Fortunately for humanity, each man is only himself and only the genius is given the ability to be others as well' (1991: 19). Pessoa must know what he is talking about, as he himself put that assertion to successful test by spawning 'heteronyms' (seventy-two altogether!): writing different poems under different names, each of those names standing for a person with a style, biography and personality of his own. *The Book of Disquiet* was penned under the name of Bernardo Soares, whom Pessoa described as a 'mutilation of my personality'.

RR Good you brought this up. I would be the last person to assert the existence of a self-identical, let alone immutable

Cartesian subject that interacts with the world, be it on its own terms or not. This is why I speak about 'interiority', not subjectivity. The interiority of other people is what mind-readers claim to have access to, and in that sense it is separate from my outside. However, interiority is not an 'inner self' – it might rather be conceived as the space within which 'self' happens, as a process. And this self is indeed a symphony (or, in the worst cases, a cacophony) – just as I was speaking about 'music' as the part of language that cannot be described in physicalist terms, there is an element of such music present in everything we think, say and do. But the interiority of each of us has a different acoustic, so to say. Think of the experience of your own voice within your head, and how you hear it from a recording. The latter is its externality, different and – in my case at least – somehow much less pleasant than what is heard inside. Nonetheless, the people who love you and love your voice can only love that unpleasant sound that you hear from the recording. This is where the gap is. Between any self-expression and any interpretation of it is this gap, and that is where speech happens.

Who else to remind us of this than Fernando Pessoa, whose proper name means 'person' in Portuguese, and who has so many 'heteronyms', as he called them: poets of quite different dispositions co-habiting his interiority, each with his own distinct voice? We all have this Bakhtinian heteroglossia within us, it is just that Pessoa listened more carefully than most others.

But let me give you another example. There is one particularly impressive short story in James Joyce's *Dubliners*, called 'The Counterparts'. Here we see Farrington, an underdog, a humiliated clerk, being abused by his boss – not without reason, to be fair, but it is still with him that our sympathies reside. Farrington's day continues, predictably, in the pub, in the company of friends, and finally he comes home, and now he has turned himself into a brute and a veritable monster, chasing his son who, in panic, promises to say a Hail Mary for him. It takes the genius of Joyce to change the man from the victim to the oppressor under our very eyes, taking him from one extreme to the other without us noticing. I still remember my first-time reading of this story, when the transformation struck me as a complete surprise, and yet I had to admit the process had proceeded seamlessly, and also that it was not possible to pinpoint the exact moment where the shift took place.

Why I am talking about this is because Farrington's interiority, throughout this process, hasn't changed, although he looks to us a completely different person, the counterpart of his initially presented self, at the end of the story. This is precisely why the gap is always present: there is no strict correspondence here. Farrington's continuous interior process seems to us, readers and outsiders, to express itself as two extremes of human behaviour at different instances – he, however, most likely seems to himself just as himself at both times.

3

Performing Selves

Rein Raud There was another important topic you mentioned, among other things, not so long ago: how the social setting relates to the self: bringing out certain aspects in it, downgrading others. Perhaps we should speak about social performance in this context, rather than self-expression or efforts to bring what is taking place within to the outside in as pure a form as possible. The emergence of the social 'I' has intermittently been analysed as a process akin to performance since the groundbreaking work of Erving Goffman (1959), and recently, under the influence of Jeffrey C. Alexander (2006), this view is again gaining more ground. So maybe it is indeed more fruitful to add an interaction with the audience to our perspective on selfhood. Indeed, coming into being and constantly reshaped at the borders of interiority, any self is entangled in multiple relationships at every given moment, some of these past and some present, some conscious and some not necessarily, some hostile and some built on mutual dependence, some paramount and some just formed and dissolved in passing. Relationships with other people, or, to be precise, with their words and acts, or to be even more precise, with one's own understanding of what these words and acts mean. In this sense, the production of selfhood necessarily has to involve negotiations with all the meaningful others towards whom one's self-expression is directed, and constant correction of one's own actions whenever something seems to have gone amiss. Strategies, gambits, offensives, manoeuvres. Sometimes the game seems to be more real than what it is about.

Zygmunt Bauman   I cannot recall, alas, who wrote that, when two people, A and B, talk to each other, six persons participate: in addition to A and B, also A's image of B, B's image of A, A's image of B's image of A and B's image of A's image of B – but I remember finding that observation, many years ago, tremendously accurate and pertinent. You add, and rightly, a considerable complexity to that shocking yet all the same straightforward, picture of the 'elementary particle' of the self that nevertheless contains already an encounter between autonomous subjects – and you do that by introducing a third subject to the dyad: that 'third' who by its mere appearance saps and contaminates the pristine innocence of the 'moral party of two' in Levinas (Bauman 2000: 110–44), or in Simmel 'deprives conflicting claims of their affective qualities' by the 'objectifying' impact of its 'disinterestedness' – and by the same token clears the site for norms, laws, ethical rules and courts of justice (Simmel 1950: 143–53). You also, consistently, suggest that the natural habitat in which formation (and re-formation!) of the self occurs is 'interaction with the audience' rather than as unaccompanied solo performance, let alone a mental self-vivisection.

However: of what does that 'audience' consist, and how does it come into being? George Herbert Mead has written of the role of 'significant others' in composing that 'me' which offers the pattern with which the 'I' is, and/or feels, bound to reckon – and to which that 'I' either surrenders or clashes and wrestles (Mead 1972). This, however, is another model of an 'elementary cell' of the interaction leading to self-formation; a specific model, attempting to grasp the self's dynamics – in a society marked by a morphology significantly distinct from the one typical of contemporary forms of human togetherness; a model made to the measure of societies of *communities* rather than *networks*, of individuals living in a 'linear' rather than 'pointillist' time, and oriented towards a self-contained area of physical proximity, and not as nowadays to electronic 'information highways'; as well as a model of socialization targeted at the self's 'authenticity' rather than its flexibility. All in all, that model does not account for the self being 'at *every* given moment', as you put it, 'entangled in *multiple* relationships' (and, let me add, most of those relationships being conspicuous for their fluid, transient and eminently revocable, 'until-further-notice' status) – the fact that should be placed in the very centre of an investigation of the dynamics of the self once it is conducted, as ours is, in a multi-centred, deregulated, fragmented and fluid world of similarly fragmented and deregulated lives.

Apart from the changed morphology of the life setting, there is also another similarly novel phenomenon of (to invoke Marshall McLuhan's thesis) the new media being a new message. Our waking hours are nowadays divided between online and offline realms, with the share of the first steadily rising at the expense of the second. The two realms differ considerably, and there are reasons to expect considerably different impacts which they might exert on the self-formation and self-reformation processes. Signals they emit and strategies they prompt are not immediately compatible; in some respects, they are at loggerheads with each other.

A most salient difference between the two realms (and probably the most responsible for the spectacular success and forest-fire-style expansion of the electronic substitution for the face-to-face) is in the degree of comfort and convenience of the interaction with the audiences on offer. Mead's negotiations between 'me' and 'I', and the labour involved in the self obtaining the social recognition it needs and claims, have been simplified and facilitated online beyond recognition, as the compromises and capitulations they inevitably require now and then in their offline version are inside the online realm reduced to a minimum, if not staved off altogether – thanks to the expedient of fast, facile and painless entry and exit from networks, in stark opposition to the protracted, cumbersome and thorny offline procedures. If negotiations are too awkward and the strings attached too tight for the self's liking or endurance, there are oodles of other 'networks' to which the self's applications to join, complete with its allegiance, can be readdressed.

Besides, there is an (increasingly popular, and already commonly as well as matter-of-factly adopted) option of maintaining *simultaneously* those 'multiple relationships' to which you point, each calling for a somewhat modified and sometimes even totally different self, or at any rate its totally different representation. The result is the cancellation of the postulates of coherence and

consistency, once among the sternest demands, and the most difficult to cope with, that self-formation would posit. Instead of the
issue of the 'presentation of self in public', online users confront
the problem of 'presentation of self in *publics*' – a fateful change
that simultaneously complicates and tremendously facilitates their
task. The processes of self-formation, self-presentation and self-
negotiation are in the online realm stripped of the most discom-
forting among their associated risks. The bets can be hedged, as
they indeed are, even if with but a mixed success.

In short, the issue of the dynamics of self seems to be moving/
drifting from the realm of cognitive and moral spaces to that of
the aesthetic (for more discussion, see Bauman 2000: 145–85).

RR   The question of how the audience is constituted is a good
one, and you are certainly right that they are heterogeneous most
of the time. A student raising her or his hand and asking a question after the lecture is most definitely at least as conscious of
fellow students as s/he is of the professor to whom the question
is addressed. So in some countries there are no questions asked,
because nobody wishes to look stupid, and in other countries there
are lots of questions asked precisely for the same reason. However,
in both cases, what indeed matters more is not the actual expectations of fellow students, but the idea of the acting self of what
these expectations are – A's image of B's image of A, as you put
it. Not that A would not wish to challenge and manipulate it,
quite to the contrary. Just like on stage or screen, the better part
of an actor's performance depends on her or his ability to give us
what we don't know to expect; I would say that successful and
convincing self-presentations both conform to and challenge the
images that their recipients anticipate. Friedrich Schleiermacher
once divided all texts into three kinds: the classical, which are
productive in their form; the original, innovative in their ideas;
and those of genius, which do both at the same time (1998: 13).
Most texts fall into one of the first two categories, because they
are more functional, providing their recipients with clear implicit
guides to approaching them. Evidently this is also why a genius is
usually likely to be misunderstood. But isn't it true that the same
applies to self-presentations everywhere? Either they conform to
a certain expectable pattern of behaviour, which facilitates the
reception of what they want to say, or do not, which initially

forces their audiences to look for a key, a code for how to interpret them. In contemporary society, however, most such erratic behaviour has already been classified and coded. When an artist, for example, dresses extravagantly or a poet appears at a public function more than slightly intoxicated, they do not challenge accepted norms, but in fact confirm them. In Schleiermacher's terms, you can be classical or original, but there is no room for genius. For quite some time, those who want to 'differ' have had to buy their gear in a chain store. Individuality has, to a significant extent, become a matter of choice between brands. Interesting choice of term, brand – a contemporary version of the brand marks on cattle to differentiate the livestock of one owner from that of another. Now worn with pride and at considerable expense. And making the wearers 'readable' to their peers.

ZB Schleiermacher's 'genius', just as Kafka's 'Messiah', 'comes the day after his arrival', which simply means, in an only slightly veneered-over tautological way, that either they are recognized as such *retrospectively* – or it never occurs to us to assign such names to them. Following routine means *invisibility*, 'hiding in the light', in the style of the Heideggerian 'das Man' or Sartrean 'l'on'. Breaking the routine, on the other hand, assures *visibility* solely of a Herostratus' sort; even if for a quite different reason, no one except dedicated Manicheans would call a meddlesome disturber of the routine a 'genius', let alone a 'Messiah'. The idea of a 'genius misunderstood' sounds to me therefore like a pleonasm – unless you add to that misunderstanding a qualifier: 'temporary', 'thus far' or 'until further notice'. After all, one can be 'innovative' and 'original' in oodles of ways, most of which prove blind alleys, false dawns or gambits leading astray. Which manifestation of originality is a mark of genius and which is no more than another of all-too-common blunders is decided retrospectively, and there is no time limit attached to that decision and its eventual revisions. The pattern set by a solitary eccentric's innovation needs first to transmogrify into a routine for the weirdo to be ushered into the 'genius' class through the gate reserved for the 'precursors', 'harbingers', 'trail blazers' and 'pioneers' – or indeed 'prophets'.

   You are right when noticing that the first two of Schleiermacher's varieties are nowadays separated more in conceptual speculations than social practice. Our times are marked on one hand by the growing flexibility and frailty as well as shortening life-expectation of routines, and on the other by codification as well as standardization of routine breaking. Simmel was the first analyst to presage the present-day climax of those interconnected processes; he insisted that for human beings everywhere 'similarity, as fact or as tendency, is no less important than difference. In the most varied forms, both are the great principles of all external and internal development. In fact, the cultural history of mankind can be conceived as the history of the struggles and conciliatory attempts between the two' (1950: 30). And in his seminal study of fashion he demonstrated how, in that practice, the clash between equally strong propulsions – one to joining up and the other to standing out – is sought to be suspended in a string of transient, short-lived armistices.

In our liquid modern world of consumers guided by consumerist markets, ephemeral and evanescent armistices followed by brief intervals of cooperation have turned into a norm – to the extent of effacing, for all practical intents and purposes, the enmity of 'belonging' and 'breaking out'. In the pattern-setting circles and in the masses of pattern-followers 'belonging' is conditional on a perpetual readiness and ability to 'break out'. Obedience to the continuous meanderings of fashion and the promptness in following them serve simultaneously both needs – of similarity and difference. The opposites have been thereby reconciled; paradoxically, though, the constant tension between them is an inseparable trait of their mode of cohabitation.

RR   Well, this is not quite what I meant. In spite of the cultural industries' efforts to standardize the extraordinary, the yearning for it has not gone away, no matter how quickly ever newer trends replace the most recent ones. And I think this is one of the things we have to keep in mind when we approach online performances of selfhood. My offline versions are always predetermined by a number of factors I have little or no influence upon – my age, my gender, my limited means – and their success or failure is always the outcome of encounters with very particular audiences, the people of my here and now. Even through the filter of TV, in order to achieve what David Foster Wallace has called 'watchableness', the 'most significant quality of truly alive persons' (1998: 26), and also the ultimate prerequisite of visual success, I have to adjust and modify myself to a degree sometimes beyond my reach. My online versions, however, are much more completely the manifestations of my own will, my own image of who I am. Needless to say, these do not develop in an empty space, but reflect the ideals and ideas of the surrounding world. For example, social networks are full of sad and ridiculous pictures – some of them posters' own 'selfies', others circulated as satire – of what people think makes them 'sexy'. We can perceive the utterly inhuman character of the standard of 'sexy' precisely where it fails, not where it is deployed successfully and thereby naturalized so that its voluntary character remains hidden. Nonetheless, the construction of my internet avatars gives me far greater possibilities than offline reality. I can be who I want to be. This may be an upgraded representation of who I am in my offline life, or a completely fictional character, or something in-between, a constructed image of how I want to appear – a true Deleuzian 'body without organs'. I may be the one who posts, but I become what is posted.

ZB   Or at least I assume that much, having acquired the grounds to believe that this 'becoming' has indeed taken place – thanks to the additional facilities which the online universe offers but the offline realities staunchly deny. The facilities in question are the 'echo chambers' or 'halls of mirrors' already mentioned before. In the online world, I can cut for myself a niche surrounded by impermeable walls, a feat inconceivable in the offline universe, and feel free and safe in such shelter; bah! I feel fully and truly in control of the choice of a self, complete with all its paraphernalia, their presentation and social acceptance. And I can accomplish that feat with the simple device of a 'delete' or 'escape' key.

   As Jean-Claude Kaufmann sums up the psychological effect of such setting: 'An individual armed with a mouse imagines that [s/he] is in complete and absolute control of [his/her] social contacts...All the usual obstacles appear to have vanished, and a world of endless possibilities opens up...A [woman or man] on the net is like a child who has been let loose in a sweetshop' (2012: 7).

RR   But is that really such a problem? Maybe we should see this as another step in the liberation process that has evolved from a rigid class system towards a merit-based and much more egalitarian community of individuals. Maybe our IT-infused reality relates to the pre-computer era in the same way as a completely furnished urban apartment relates to a traditional farmhouse, with a dry toilet outside and all housework done by hand. Of course, handmade pies taste better, but are they worth all the trouble – and the relinquished careers of the housewives who bake them? Perhaps we should look at the situation with a move in mind akin to Jacques Derrida's cancellation of the opposition between voice and writing (1997: 8–9)? For Derrida, 'writing', although in its current sense a phenomenon historically much later than speech, is in fact the primordial activity, of which speech is but a variation. So maybe avatar construction is in fact closer to the essence of self-performance, which has been restricted by many material factors before the advent of the internet? Take art, for example. It is in the nature of cultural practices to have to be redefined with any new endorsed and productive paradigm change. With the advent of modern and contemporary art, traditional definitions were rendered obsolete, but the new definitions nonetheless had to tackle something essential, something that would encompass both the older forms of art and the new ones that had come into being as a form of opposition to them. So maybe, instead of problematizing the online life-forms of internet selfhood, we should look for something that unites avatar construction with previous genres of self-presentation? And perhaps even celebrate the new and liberating possibilities of constantly advancing technology?

ZB Perhaps it wouldn't 'be a problem' if the online world securely ensconced in its technological shelter were the only universe we inhabit. In such a case, we would hardly discover that living in it is a 'problem'. This is not, however, how our condition presents itself to us and how we experience it: we inhabit currently *two* universes, online and offline, each with its own rules, behavioural codes and set of options, mutually contradictory and irreconcilable in quite a few respects – but nowadays we are all indefatigable commuters, shuttling many times a day from one universe to the other and back, and all too often marooned in both simultaneously. The two universes may be irreconcilable, but we can't help trying incessantly that uncanny job of reconciliation. The errors of confusing the demands of one universe with those of another are unavoidable, and all too often harmful to both self-esteem and interpersonal relations: to one's own self and its public perception and evaluation. Besides, the advantages of the relative effortlessness of online life when compared with the trials and tribulations of the troublesome offline existence causes internet users to gradually denigrate and de-learn (or fail to appropriate in the first place) the skills required to cope with offline demands – their resulting impairment making those demands look yet more daunting and fearsome, off-putting and repulsive.

RR I am not even so sure about two universes any longer, when I look at someone crossing a street and texting at the same time, or doing the same in the company of friends. The borders of online and offline lives are getting hazier with every new invention, so we most likely end up with just one world which is really neither. Personally, still, I am not as optimistic as Google Glasses promoters who promise that soon the field of our vision will be saturated with hyperlinks – perhaps more likely would be a situation where you would be looking at a multitude of error messages superimposed on what you see: '404 Not Found', 'Loading 23%...', 'The server is busy now. Come back later.'

Be that as it may, I can think of one more serious counterargument to the enthusiastic view of the liberating possibilities of new technology: one related to what we take 'being human' to mean. However impermanent and swiftly changing our offline life might be, online life is much more so, and it is so much easier to exit it (almost) without trace. I am not talking about searchable mega data in secret databanks at the moment, but about the easiness of changing my profile picture or of unfriending people I don't like. I am what I post, but I can edit my posts all the time. This is a bit like what you called 'echo chambers', surrounding myself only with people who agree with me. But even more than that – it presents me with the liberty to leave such an echo chamber at will and build myself a new one, if for some reason the former does not satisfy me any longer.

This, for me, is a big problem: the easy way out. Existential problems do not have to be solved, challenges do not have to be overcome – they can be discarded. Of course, we know that no final solution to a serious existential problem can ever be found. To my mind it is those interim, imperfect solutions that make us

what we are, or human beings. But if I can edit out all my imperfections instead of working on them, where does this leave me?

ZB   On that point, I couldn't agree with you more! I would,
however, add to the 'what we take "being human" to mean' also
'what we take "being happy" (or having a gratifying life) to mean'
– all the more emphatically for the misconception of that meaning
being so widespread. On oodles of occasions I have been asked
by all sorts of interviewers whether I view my life as having been
happy. I never found a better response than to quote (*toutes proportions gardées!*) the answer given by Johann Wolfgang Goethe
when he was asked, on reaching almost – though not quite – my
present age, whether he had a happy life. He replied that he had
had a happy *life*, though he couldn't recall a single happy *week*.
I believe that the easily decipherable message which his reply was
meant to – and did – convey is now, as it was then, crucial for
our understanding of the nature of happiness: namely, that the
feeling of happiness does not derive from a life free from trouble,
but from confronting life's troubles point blank and with the visor
raised – and then resisting them, fighting, solving, overwhelming...A similar thought was expressed by Goethe in one of his
poems: 'alles in der Werlt lässt sich ertragen / Nur nicht eine Reihe
von schönen Tagen' (meaning: everything in the world is endur-
able, except beautiful days in a row). The alternative to facing up
to the problems and resolving them is not happiness, but boredom,
ennui, spleen.

RR   Precisely. Remember what I said about the general mistrans-
lation of 'suffering' in Buddhist texts: bliss is similar to pain in
that in both states we would not really want the precise experience
of the present moment to go on endlessly. But isn't 'happiness' as
a practical, life-forming concept, for most people, a matter of
emulation? If, on the one hand, we agree that the word cannot
possibly denote a uniform, realistically sustainable condition
because of our biological, social and cultural limitations, but on
the other hand cannot give up the ideal of happiness as a standard
of self-realization, then the easy way out is via surrogates for
happiness.
    The idea of emulation is really not new and most certainly not
limited to material things such as the lifestyles that you can buy

in chainstores, complete with accessories. Ancient Chinese ethics traditionally operated with emulation models. The Analects of Confucius are full of statements of what 'a noble man' would do in a certain situation and the competing Daoists explain the same things about 'the wise sage'. Later poets emulated earlier poets not just in their writing, but also in their life, and so, I gather, did many of the aspiring Bohemians of *fin-de-siècle* Paris, sometimes quite consciously, it seems, emulating prescribed patterns of unhappiness and suffering that were the prerequisite of the ultimate self-realization. The same must have been true of mystics such as Thomas à Kempis who taught his followers to imitate (= emulate) Christ himself. Or recall the advice of Pascal to those who were losing faith:

> You would like to attain faith and do not know the way; you would like to cure yourself of unbelief and ask the remedy for it. Learn of those who have been bound like you, and who now stake all their possessions. These are people who know the way which you would follow, and who are cured of an ill of which you would be cured. Follow the way by which they began; by acting as if they believed, taking the holy water, having masses said, etc. Even this will naturally make you believe, and deaden your acuteness. (2003: 68)

Slavoj Žižek comments on this passage: 'Pascal's final answer, then, is: leave rational argumentation and submit yourself simply to ideological ritual, stupefy yourself by repeating the meaningless gestures, act *as if* you already believe, and the belief will come by itself' (1989: 39). The problem with this reading is that these gestures, or images, or mantras, are not meaningless. On the contrary: they are fundamental acts of signification, giving meaning, reorganizing meaning in the most profound way. And the context for performing such conversion is not necessarily ideological in the strict sense of the word. An initiate to academia pronouncing words such as 'simulacrum' or 'difference' for the first time (oh, how well I remember that) is not fundamentally different from a small-town girl articulating 'Harrods' or 'Galleries Lafayette' when she tells her friend where she is headed. The difference is not so much between the mechanisms of what is taking place, but between the background systems, the principles that this conversion-performance introduces into our lives and the changes they can produce there – just as a religious conversion of the same kind may open the road to becoming a violent fundamentalist, or a peaceful volunteer caring for the penniless.

This brings us back to the question of performance as a way of self-production. Emulation should be, by definition, its very opposite, but it is not. First of all, emulating a model is usually for the benefit of an audience, even if only one composed of the performer him-/herself. Secondly, in the most widespread forms, emulation is partial. I will never become the person in the commercial clip, just as I will never become my teacher, nor, for that matter, Christ or Elvis Presley. But I can buy myself the clothes, and quote from the same books as my teacher did. So emulation is not necessarily as total as a religious conversion would be, even though the act itself is not fundamentally different. Emulation is very much a technique of *bricolage,* to use Claude Lévi-Strauss' term for assembling heterogeneous bits and pieces into functional new wholes, which derive their unity not from their origins, but from the way they now relate to each other. This relation is precisely the kind of self that emulation can help to produce.

ZB   Let me respond in reverse order and start from the connection/opposition of emulation and self-creation.

Once more I agree that the two aspects of emulation are intertwined and possible to set apart solely as concepts but hardly in practice. Derrida has also suggested speaking of 'iteration' instead of deploying the common term 'reiteration': no apparent repetition or reproduction is fully identical with what is repeated or reproduced. Three centuries earlier Leibniz entertained the court ladies setting them a highly time-consuming yet ultimately doomed task of finding two identical leaves in the court's vast gardens. So much about the *synchronic* identity; as to the *diachronic* version of that connection/opposition – Heraclitus two millennia earlier solved the problem by observing that you can't enter the same river twice. He would be right to clarify that this rule acts both ways: neither *the river* which you enter 'again' can be 'the same' as it was the first time, nor can *you* who entered the river the first time be still the same at your second attempt.

Indeed, production of self cannot be anything but a continuing, incessant, forever inconclusive and open-ended interaction between an 'I' and (to borrow Martin Buber's distinction) either 'thou' or 'it'. From such interaction, *none* of the agents involved emerges unchanged. 'Interaction' boils down in the last resort to the interconnectedness of the agents' transformations; it can be presented as a loop of interconnected identity changes. Were it not for the dissimilarity of the agents involved, there would be neither an impulse nor the substance to their entanglement. The 'loop' is a product of the complementary actions of two agents – 'I' and the 'world' (a shorthand for the sum total of the 'not I's').

'We would not really want the present moment to go on endlessly' – you say. You might have added: neither are we *allowed* to want; as Goethe's Faust learned the hard way by facing the eternal damnation once he begged the fleeting moment 'Verweile doch! du bist so schön!' (meaning: Linger longer! You are so beautiful!). Happiness, as Freud insisted, has no staying power; it is not here to stay – let alone to stay indefinitely. Happiness is something to run to. Happiness is a *change* in the status quo – the moment of leaping away from a peculiar annoyance and putting paid to a particular exasperation; by definition, it can't overstay that moment for long. It won't survive its own prolonged presence, that Goethe's 'row of sunny days'. As a matter of fact, one could even fantasize that the longing for happiness was instilled in us in order to make us the incurably listless and transgressive, forward-looking creatures that we are.

The snag is that, while the fact of the '*state* of happiness' staying beyond our reach (perhaps even being a contradiction in terms) is the warrant and effective cause for insatiable curiosity and an unquenchable thirst for novelty, as well as an inexhaustible source of creative energy – the conviction that the state of happiness is but a daydream may well cause that curiosity and that thirst to wilt and fade; it is, however, the opposite, counterfactual convictions – the belief in its *attainability*, or at least disbelief in the ultimate vanity of efforts to force the state of happiness to stay – that is the *sine-qua-non* condition of all and any drive to improvement.

Well, God being far away, impenetrable to the meagre comprehending capacity of the mere humans and reluctant to answer their queries, we, the humans, are inclined to tinker with His DIY substitutes: Bruno Latour's 'faitishes', man-made idols to whom we impute allegedly super-human, divine provenance and connections. As happiness shares with God the qualities of aloofness,

incomprehensibility and unattainability, we, the pursuers of happiness, must settle for the faitishes of 'authorities' – as Confucius'
'noble men' or Daoist 'sages' whom you mention, Christian saints
(I suspect Thomas à Kempis went a step too far in his advice to
the faithful and could be open to the charge of blasphemy), Jewish
Tzadiks; or, closer to our times, the loquacious 'gurus' or the noisy
spokesmen for the silent ones, and in our own times the celebrated
idols or idolized celebrities of the day. What unites them over the
ages that separate them is the fact of being acknowledged as lode-
stars or road signs – authorities pronouncing on the choice of the
'right way': of the mode of life that promises to lead into a state
of happiness, however defined and denominated. In the past such
authority was assigned to teachers; currently, it belongs mostly to
personal examples. Both are 'people who know the way which
you would follow, and who are cured of an ill of which you would
be cured', as you quote from Pascal – or rather, more to the point,
people who are *acclaimed* to know the way, and whom you
believe, because of that acclamation, to have been cured of the
scourge of which you wish to be cured, and most importantly
self-cured, thanks to your willing, earnest and determined, even if
difficult and demanding, conversion to a new faith, to a new value
hierarchy and preferences, new diet, new lifestyle, or new strategy
to be deployed in entering, staying in and terminating relations
with others. Or just thanks to moving home to places you haven't
yet visited, or trying activities or relations you haven't yet tested.
As Joseph Brodsky has put it:

> you may take up changing jobs, residence, company, country,
> climate; you may take up promiscuity, alcohol, travel, cooking
> lessons, psychoanalysis...In fact, you may lump all these together,
> and for a while that may work. Until the day, of course, when you
> wake up in your bedroom amid a new family and a different wall-
> paper, in a different state and climate, with a heap of bills
> from your travel agent and your shrink, yet with the same stale
> feeling toward the light of day pouring through the window.
> (1995: 107–8)

You are also right when objecting to Žižek's reading of Pascal and
insisting that the 'gestures, or images, or mantras' obtained,
appropriated and deployed in the act of conversion 'are not
meaningless'. The rituals marking the conversion are indeed

lived-through as bestowing the heretofore lacking yet keenly desired meaning to life, at least to its nearest prospects (few if any will / dare to look further than that into the notoriously capricious future) – and that is on the authority of the multitude of their followers and of the testimony of the huge number of 'likes' recorded on their website rendition. According to the English folk wisdom, 'any port will do in a storm'. The 'storm', in the particular case of our present condition, stands for the dazing, confusing and stupefying whirlwind of fast aging revelations, prediction, auguries, counsels and commendations; any self-confidently promoted recipe for happiness may stand for a 'port' under such circumstances.

I suspect that the currently evident advantage of celebrities (people, according to the witty if caustic definition of Daniel J. Boorstin, who 'are well known for their well-knownness') over saints or sages has something to owe to their endemic transience juxtaposed with the eternity of saintliness of saints and wisdom of sages. That transience and notorious absence of a staying power better fits the experience derived from living under 'liquid modern' conditions and the present-day antipathy to long-term, let alone indefinite, commitments and irreversible choices. Another advantage of celebrities is their abstention from demanding that emulation be total and exclusive. Unlike the saints or sages, they are tolerant to tinkering – a boon for people cast in the plight of tinkers by that decree of fate called 'modern condition'.

RR   Quite some time ago, Peter Stromberg compared the celebrities of our world to deities, who mediate between us and the divine upstairs. As he writes:

Celebrities are deities because they are the most significant mediators in American consumerism; like the Christian deity Jesus Christ they are at once human and God. They are the ones who participate in two worlds, the world we all live in and the world we all aspire to. Although they started out as mortals like you and me, they live their current lives in our idea of heaven, the world that is depicted in advertisements, where people are happy, beautiful, witty, satisfied, adventurous, friendly, and so on.... The minor setbacks that do occur even in paradise – divorce, addictions, at times even a suicide – are fascinating because they reveal these celestial creatures to be just like us. (1990: 17)

Accordingly, he concludes, Americans (or any carriers of contemporary culture, for that matter) believe that 'the existence they live from day to day can be transformed – must be transformed – through the transformation of themselves. The self can be changed through consumption' (1990: 18). In that sense, consumption is no longer the satisfaction of our own needs, whether real or imaginary – it has become a somewhat Baudrillardian religious practice based on emulation. By wearing Björn Borg-label boxers, I partake of the body of Björn Borg, just as a Christian, during the Eucharist, partakes of the god's body. Albeit only in a detail (and even though no one can see), it is still a performance, but one where I am no longer the author of the script. Similarly, by using a particular brand of corn flakes I bridge my annoyingly noisy breakfast table to the cute and happy family in the commercial, so even if my own close ones do not live up to the ideal, they will still be consisting partially of the same stuff as the celestial beings who enjoy it on the other side of the TV screen.

George Carlin once suggested that commercials should be more violently realistic instead of portraying an idealized world, so that they would sound something like 'Hey, Dad, when you get finished punchin' Mom, gimme some more of that shit with the raisins in it, will ya?' (2001: 53). But it is not the corn flakes that are sold in advertising; it is the religious moment of identification. I may want a realistic bridge to the reality of the product when it is being sold to me on the ground of its functional properties – for example, if it is a washing detergent or an electric drill. An angelic girl would convince me less of the superiority of such a product than a knowledgeable housewife with the right questions or an experienced workman with oily hands. However, the breakfast cereal (unless it is sold to me as particularly healthy or some such) competes with others of its kind for this added symbolic value rather than for its taste quality. In the world of fashion – or the arts, as Pierre Bourdieu has argued (1993: 76–7) – the process may even work in the opposite direction: the new colour is not promoted by the fashion house because it is about to become fashionable – it is about to become fashionable because that particular fashion house promotes it.

What does this do to someone who genuinely does not like this colour? You have got a choice, as usual: either you perform the movement that puts you slightly ahead of others, and thereby increase its momentum, or you conscientiously object. Can you do *that* without performing? I don't think so. On a minimal scene within myself, I still have to act this minimal piece to myself: I am the one who refused to go along with the choice of the masses. Does this not, in fact, require an even more convincing show than the (possibly Pascalian) endorsement of any latest trend?

Let me add immediately that if that is so – if there is no choice – then we have to think about performance in ethically completely neutral terms. There is nothing wrong with doing it: as long as we are ourselves, it is like breathing. If, by performing my choice to myself, I make it possible to stand by the values and principles that I hold dear, then the little division of myself into an actor and an audience serves a worthwhile goal. You spoke a little earlier of Mead and his distinction between 'I' and 'me', Charles S. Peirce saw 'me' in dialogue with an internal 'you', and sociologists often speak about 'significant others' whom 'I' has internalized to the point that they have become constituents of its selfhood. If we accept that the self is internally dialogical or polylogical, then it has to be performing itself constantly, hasn't it? We also agreed before that, even if the self is in reality acting before an audience, there is a difference between what actually takes place and the internal performance of itself before the audience it imagines. What we have to note, however, is that the efficacy of that performance depends on the endorsement of the internal audience just as much as the external one. Imagine a really talented musician, who is so excessively self-critical that, no matter how long the audience applauds, she still thinks they are just doing this out of courtesy, pretending not to have noticed her utterly dismal failure.

ZB 'Self' is a determinant as much as a product of interaction. That most private of human possessions is also the one most dependent on human sociality. If not for being social animals, we would probably never have come across the idea that we are or have 'selves'. It is in interaction with others (as you rightly point out those 'out there', as well as those already incorporated as 'significant others' and set inside the self in a perpetual court session in the unending 'Me' vs 'I' trial) that the awareness of 'having a self' or indeed of 'being a self' dawns upon us and the life-long labour of building and rebuilding identities is conducted.

As you accurately put it, 'as long as we are ourselves, it is like breathing'.

In the openings of interaction, presentation of 'Self' plays the role of a visiting card: a token of self-introduction (in nineteenth-century novels, one of the most frequent motifs was people begging their acquaintances 'to introduce' them to this or that attractive woman or this or that influential man; now, in a society where tokens of identities are stored and sold in shops, introductions tend to be 'do it yourself' tasks – with fashions taking over the office of gatekeepers). Visiting cards need to be written in whatever passes currently for vernacular, and legibly – otherwise they'd fail their purpose. Nowadays such cards are printed on the body, in a sartorial lingo or the patois of demeanour and countenance – rather than held, as the visiting cards of yore, in a waistcoat pocket, to be drawn out on some occasions and kept inside ready to be drawn on all others. The contemporary equivalents of the old-style visiting cards are endowed with an additional task of selecting, after the pattern of smart missiles, their targets – the addressees to whom they send the invitation to interact – and the parallel task of keeping at a distance the others, to whom the invitation would rather not be extended. Looked at from the opposite, the addressees', side, they are either pleas for admission, or announcements of unwillingness to join; selves, as it were, need to combine those two facilities – just as that anecdotal English shipwreck marooned on an uninhabited island, who felt the need to build two hovels in addition to the hut he called his home: one accommodating a club to be visited each evening, and another inside which he was resolute never to set his foot.

Well, celebrities are not deities; they, together with their visible/ audible/tangible signifiers, have merely replaced the saints and their necklace or badge likenesses as arguably the easiest and most commonly recognizable tokens of self's identity – having shed on the way the 'sanctity connection' of their antecedents. What unite the deities with celebrities are the claims and tokens of belonging that they represent; all other similarities, if there are any, are (to borrow the phrase deployed by lawyer-shy film producers) 'purely accidental'. But it is their difference that makes the difference: it is the fact of replacing that casts most light on the profound change in the strategies of the self's production that has occurred in our 'liquid-modern' times – a change reflecting alterations in the substance and strategy of sociality and the interplay of individuality and belonging.

In an essay titled 'From Martyr to Hero, and from Hero to Celebrity', I wrote:

> By contrast with the case of martyrs or heroes, whose fame was derived from their deeds and whose flame was kept alive in order to commemorate those deeds and so to restate and reaffirm their lasting importance, the *reasons* which brought celebrities into the limelight are the least important causes of their 'knownness'. The decisive factor here is their *notoriety*, the abundance of their images and the frequency with which their names are mentioned in public broadcasts and private conversations...Like martyrs and heroes, they provide a sort of glue that brings and holds together otherwise diffuse and scattered aggregates of people; one would be tempted to say that nowadays they are the principal factors generating communities were not communities in question not only imagined, as in the society of the solid modern era, but also imaginary, apparition-like; and above all loosely knit, frail, volatile, and recognized as ephemeral. It is mostly for that reason that celebrities are so comfortably at home in the liquid modern setting: liquid modernity is their natural ecological niche. (2005: 49–50)

Celebrities do not demand unconditional commitment and loyalty – those two requirements that put so many individuals immersed in the liquid-modern world off the old-style, tightly knit communities, and prompt them to choose instead 'networks', distinguished by the extreme facility of connecting and disconnecting, joining and quitting. Neither do the celebrities claim exclusive rights to being emulated; however enthusiastic and dedicated at the moment the wearers of T-shirts with the likeness of a celebrity A emblazoned on them are, there is always room in the wearer's wardrobe for T-shirts adorned with the effigies of celebrities B, C and any number of others. Joining the bevy of a celebrity's adulators does not feel as surrender of one's freedom – but as testimony to, and reassuring confirmation and reassertion of, the flatterer's freedom. No mortgaging of one's individual future is involved – the kind of assurance the individuals-by-decree value highly and cherish.

4

Self-Realization

Rein Raud   This brings us to another circle of problems, that of self-realization. We have spoken so far about the self as an entity within a static context, but let's now introduce a broader time-frame, a personal as well as a social one. It is one thing to try emulating an ideal that is readily available for the purpose, but most of the time self-realization is a lengthy process that needs discipline, a lot of work, and yields no instant gratification. The reward, if any, is always on the horizon. And yet, it seems, quite a few people normally think self-realization in the long run is more important than the immediate enjoyment of the present. 'Plant a tree, build a house, raise a son', as the saying goes.

Zygmunt Bauman   Reward 'is always on the horizon' – meaning, I guess: 'already in sight, but not yet within reach'; so you say, and I agree. But what is seen as the reward for the self-realization labours, that un-ending chase of the perpetually receding horizon? Is it still something akin to Jean-Paul Sartre's 'projet de la vie', a model selected fairly early on 'once for all', and once selected held fast and bound to be constructed patiently floor by floor, brick by brick, through an entire life and – after the pattern of gyro-scopes installed on ocean-going ships – keeping the self-builder on track against all odds? A pre-designed model, of a shape known/projected or adumbrated in advance in its entirety by us, craftsmen of the art of life, *before* we start in earnest on the labour of self-realization with a 'road map' in hand? Or even a model not yet visualized in its entirety, still somewhat misty and spattered with too many blank spots – but spots that we hope nevertheless will be filled as the labour proceeds: spots which we are determined to fill once and for all in the time to come? I don't think so.

I believe that the meaning most people tend to insert in the present-day version of the 'self-realization' idea, updated as it has been for the liquid-modern times, is more akin to the recommendation ascribed to Oliver Cromwell: 'put your trust in God; but mind to keep your powder dry'. Or, to express the same maxim in a modernized idiom, 'hedge your bets and keep your options open'. What guides the 'self-realization' efforts nowadays most commonly is not so much the crossing of t's and dotting of i's on a pre-destined and firmly embraced, as well as tenaciously and systematically followed, model of the self – but keeping it unfinished, forever pliable, leaving plenty of room for experimenting with its alternatives – known or yet unknown, but expected to emerge and be learned. What guides those efforts is *fear of fixing*, rather than *desire to reach the finishing line*. The liquid modern condition puts a premium on flexibility; and, willy-nilly, we obey.

The now outdated idea of 'self-realization' was coined to serve a relatively stable (that is, if compared to the length of individual life-expectancy), slowly changing world, guided by relatively durable, slowly – if at all – changing ethical principles, value hierarchies and strategic precepts. In that world, one could hope that the setting in which the action, however lengthy, was undertaken, wouldn't alter significantly before bringing its intended result. In such a world such expectation 'made sense'; when projected upon life, it also made sense of looking far ahead, and of long-term, fixed-goal oriented planning – as well as of consistency and unflinching determination in pursuing the fulfillment of plans to their preconceived end. The updated, liquid-modern idea of 'self-realization' is moulded, however, to serve the world in which the life-expectancy of all, or almost all, relevant ingredients of the individual life-setting (such as businesses, terms of trade, political institutions and programmes, cherished values, distinctions between *comme il faut* and *comme il ne faut pas*, dominant and/ or coveted life styles, etc.) is shrinking at a continuously accelerating pace – the length of the individual life-expectancy being the sole exception to that well-nigh universal rule. Flexibility – not consistency; willingness and ability to change destinations and vehicles in the course of the life journey – not holding to acquired beliefs and habits; all in all, forgetting rather than memorizing: these are the slogans of the day. Working not so much towards a distant ideal state, but making the best out of the current, endemically transient, opportunities. As in the famous (some say infamous) adage of Eduard Bernstein, the first 'revisionist': 'the final goal of socialism is nothing to me, the movement is everything' (1993: 190). It is indeed tempting to designate the present-day practice of self-realization as 'revisionist'.

RR I am sorry to hear you consider the idea of self-realization outdated. Of course I can understand why you say that, within the liquid settings of the present, it is no longer possible to rely on an idea of stability extending into the future as we could just a few decades ago. Indeed, a Japanese bank commercial from 1972, quoted by David Plath (1980: 89), proposed a lifelong engagement to someone who has just started work in a company, with all of the important life-events mapped out, such as the birth of the son at the age of 26 and the daughter at 30, up to the daughter's wedding and a trip to Europe a few years after retirement. The idea was that you paid the bank regularly and larger sums would be made available to you at these pre-agreed moments when you would actually need them to pay for the wedding and the trip, or college fees and so on. So you only have to sign once and your whole life is outlined for you – after that, you just get on with it. This reminds me of a sentence, dropped in passing by Marilyn Strathern, a thought that is just as cruel as it is accurate: it is the middle class that makes a project out of life (1992: ix). Indeed, those 'below' the middle cannot afford to consider their lives in terms of a project, because they are constantly engaged in a struggle to survive in the first place, while those 'above' do not need to make long-term goal commitments, because the basic reward – financial freedom that allows them to do whatever they want on the spur of the moment – is no longer a problem for them.

Well, you are certainly right in that at this moment no bank would be likely to advertise such outlined futures any longer, and rarely would anyone signing a job contract seriously think that this was for life. But I don't think this liquidity has actually made self-realization as such obsolete – it has just shifted its location elsewhere. You have described yourself how, during the structural changes of capitalist society, consumption has displaced work as the mode of exercising individual freedom (Bauman 1988: 74). However, this, too, is not quite what I have in mind. I can understand your pessimism even about 'a model not yet visualized in its entirety, still somewhat misty and spattered with too many blank spots'. And yes, social practice does seem to confirm that everything people do is patterned on a video game with a 'restart' button rather than a confident stride with which to walk through life doing things 'my way', as Sinatra once classically announced. People drift from relationship to relationship, move house with fairly little sentiment and even jump from one political party to another rather easily, so that it does seem outdated to talk about a process of self-realization that is going on.

And yet.

Perhaps your quotation of Bernstein will be more revealing if we apply it to the societies that have actually accomplished socialism, not necessarily in a Marxist understanding of the word, as a result of a violent revolution that changes quantity into quality, but in a quiet and strictly ethical way. I mean the Nordic countries that have been governed by social-democratic governments in the past for significant, formative periods, so that even though some of them have had more right-wing politicians in steering positions, they have not changed the basic Nordic ethos with its egalitarian, individualist, consensus-yearning approach to problem-solving. I would say that if the success of a country could be measured by the level of how its resources are used for the benefit of its inhabitants, the Nordic countries have done quite spectacularly, and I don't mean Norwegian oil, which is a rather late development. Take Finland, for example, with its hostile climate, low population density, a language difficult for foreigners and no considerable riches in the bowels of the Earth. And yet it is a country that has more to offer to its people than many others with much more natural potential.

If we look at Nordic political process, then this phrase of Bernstein comes to mind rather quickly. In order to move towards a social ideal, you cannot know in advance what it is like. There is no final destination. But moving towards it is nonetheless the most important thing. If you do that, you cannot pretend to be *already* someone else, a naturalized citizen of the new world, Lenin's 'new man'. Yes, you may have your ideas of what you want to become, and what others want to become. The others may share a part of your ideas, and reject another part. So the movement towards the ideal changes your vision of what the ideal is. And as soon as you have got somewhere, you immediately notice other things that have to be done in order to be yet closer to what your ideal looks like now – some of these may be problems produced by your solution, others just things you may have overlooked previously or which have only just become salient.

Thus we have two different stimuli at work here. On the one hand, the idea is to transform society, to be constantly on the move – on the other, however, it is precisely the absence of a fixed long-term ideological vision to be followed that has ensured the success of this movement. Road maps towards interim goals, yes, but not a blueprint of a total social building that has to be erected no matter what. And this is not quite what 'democracy' as such means, because a democracy can just as well take place in a site of struggle between incompatible ways of political thinking. In the Nordic societies, however, the movement follows certain agreed principles, a certain logic that is not to be abandoned, although this logic can create divergent and unpredictable social outcomes. In fact, these societies, even though they share quite a lot, are also vastly different, and not only because of the general dispositions of the people, but because of the political microchoices they have made. Yet a Nordic conservative would normally not argue for 'traditional family values' meaning that women should take up their role at home and not be the active and equal participants in social life they are.

So what is the point of this rather long aside? Maybe we might approach the problematic of self-realization from the same premises: not as fulfilling a programme, following a set life course, a path of my own invention or a trajectory prescribed to me, but as a movement without a final destination, yet governed by certain principles that I have chosen for myself and will abide by – and if something happens that puts them in contradiction, then I will have to choose again, choose between them. I want to realize myself, yet I don't know who I am: a starting point that both Socrates and Śākyamuni should be able to endorse.

ZB 'Movement without a final destination, yet governed by certain principles that I have chosen for myself and will abide by' – yes, of course! I can hardly disagree. But all the same, is not *self*-realization a myth heavily exploited nowadays by the currently hegemonic neo-liberal ideology to cover up the manipulation of 'fate' – eminently external circumstances beyond my control – by neo-liberal politics, a manipulation aimed at a concentrated assault upon the space left to the discretion of the character and its capacity for manoeuvre? Hasn't the strategy discovered by Michel Crozier exactly half a century ago (1964) in the practices of French bureaucracy – a strategy of untying one's own hands while tying up the hands of others – proved to be in the flow of time an anticipatory insight into the radically uneven distribution of the chances of self-realization – produced in our society of individualized consumers by the 'soft' rather than 'hard' power, by carrot-and-stick instead of bare-faced coercion? Can we really rise up to the neo-liberal demand to resolve individually, with individually possessed and commanded resources, life problems that are socially generated? To rise from the status of individuals-*de-jure* to that of individuals-*de-facto*?! Well, some among us – few, and a shrinking few – sometimes can. Most of us, most of the time, cannot.

Sorbonne economist Daniel Cohen writes:

> Working in a Fordist factory of old, a worker is always a worker ('providing he does not drink', as Ford said), whatever trajectory he follows. In the world starting today, the risk of 'losing everything' is permanent. The high-class professional, owner of 'unique' knowledge, may brutally descend into incompetence with the appearance of new technology; a 'specific' worker is, by definition, one that risks everything in case his company goes bankrupt or decides to make its employees redundant. Finally, the third kind of capital, collected in the course of individual life, can be lost when the workers are permanently excluded from the labour market and fall into the vicious circle of poverty and desocialisation. (1999: 91)

Are we not all in the process of being relegated, or becoming frightened by a real prospect of being relegated, to Guy Standing's 'precariat' (2011) – a populous and fast-growing assembly of individuals who are allowed to settle, whenever and wherever they do, for no longer than 'until further notice' – that is, if a notice is at all given before the blow is delivered?

Those few (mostly new global elite) who manage to stay among the beneficiaries rather than fall among the losers tend, as Luc Boltanski and Eve Chiapello suggest, to replace *savoir-faire* with *savoir-vivre* – 'stressing versatility, job flexibility and the ability to learn and adapt to new duties, rather than possession of an occupation and established qualifications, but also the capacity for engagement, communication and relational qualities' (2007: 89). At the other end of the social spectrum, there are parents with worry in their eyes as they:

> sit around a dinner table littered with more bills than dollar bills, trying to figure out whom to pay and how to save...Most people want to work. It is a basic human desire: to make a way, to provide for one's self and one's loved ones, to advance...But it is easy to see how people can have that hope thrashed out of them, by having to wrestle with the most wrenching of questions: how to make do when you work for less than you can live on? (Blow 2014b)

On some other occasion, I suggested that people-on-the-move in our liquid-modern world can be roughly split into two large categories: tourists and vagabonds; tourists are vagabonds by free and joyous choice, whereas the vagabonds are tourists by feared and resented, yet indomitable, necessity. Though for starkly different reasons, none of the two categories can and/or will stand still for long.

Against the background of a society in which celebrities currently in the limelight take over the role of life-guides from moral authorities and morality teachers, the lofty proposal of individually operated self-realization may survive as a craving of well-wishing *Schöngeisten* (aesthetes) – a yearning myopically and carelessly oblivious to the harsh realities of a society pre-setting the odds against self-autonomy, self-determination and self-assertion; against being obstinately, tenaciously, and above all successfully 'governed by certain principles that I have chosen for myself and will abide by'. This does not mean that the desire cannot be followed – but it does mean that for most people and most of the time following it stays stubbornly, frustratingly and cruelly beyond their ken. As an inveterate and probably incurable sociologist, I am inclined to conclude that, philosophically, *sub specie aeternitatis*, the Socratic strategy for meaningful life was from the start, and continues to be, right – but that also from the start, and especially in the present-day society, the probability of practising it willingly and effectively stays abominably low.

Though I agree with you, wholeheartedly, that the Nordic societies, trying earnestly as they do to resist the pressures of the neo-liberal ideological hegemony and to squeeze away the toxin of its personally addressed double-faced, hypocritical messages, demonstrate that the possibility of bringing empirical realities nearer the standards set by moral truth remains viable. I only wish that we prove them to be an avant-garde blazing the trails for us, the rest, to follow – rather than a local aberration.

RR   Perhaps we should indeed make a distinction here between how things are, and how we think they ought to be. But why only *sub specie aeternitatis*? The beginning of what you just said reminds me of Epictetus and his caution not to let ourselves be worried about things utterly beyond our control. The question is, where do these begin? In a democracy, at least, we should be able to think that the rules of social organization are, in principle, of our own making and not the manifestations of natural laws, although I, too, have met quite a few neo-liberals who tell me that greed and competition are basic, essential features of human nature, and an economic system that is built on them is thus ideal in that it inherently reflects who we are. With this, I disagree. Looking at the societies and cultures of the world and their historical development, one cannot assert anything about essential human nature – we only are who we are just now, in our present circumstances, and there is also no reason why we should stay that way, even though most of us would probably have different opinions on what we should retain and what is better left behind. Accordingly, if we find something at fault in the present socio-cultural mechanics, something that makes it impossible to act on the principles we consider philosophically right, then we have to do what we can to move these circumstances in the direction where such principles will be possible and viable choices for everyone who believes in them. Again, remember that there is no ideal out there that cannot be improved on when need be.

Most of the time, we do not even need a revolution for that. I cannot speak about the more pressing needs of the family in the dead end that your quote from Charles M. Blow describes, because a more complex solution is needed for that, but when we think of the expert worker whose skills might be outdated by the advance of a new technology – and indeed this is a clear and present danger to which very many people are constantly exposed – then this could most likely be solved by certain changes in the education system. Steps taken in the opposite direction from that in which the European university seems to be heading at the moment, I am sorry to say. For example, according to Frans van Vught of the European Centre for Strategic Management of Universities, 'the European Union needs more graduates and it needs these graduates to be directly employable. So the massification of European higher education will need to continue and enrolments will need to continue to grow' (2009: 25), the primary task of universities being the production of 'larger numbers of employable knowledge workers' (2009: 23). In my opinion, this is complete nonsense. When education is coupled to job qualifications, it can inescapably serve only the needs of the system, not of the person who is educated. Moreover, the primary performance criterion for universities is efficiency: more graduates, and more quickly. As if the development of a human being were not a process that goes on at a slower pace, and includes exposure to multiple different and contradictory streams of information as well as insoluble eternal questions and personal challenges. All that is, of course, 'inefficient', so universities are stripping their curricula of most things that are not directly relevant to the imaginary future jobs of their graduates. The problem is just that these jobs may have become redundant already by the time the students actually finish their studies and have to embark on career paths that had not even been there when the university bureaucrats designed their very 'efficient' syllabus. So it is no wonder that the proclaimed goals of all these constantly on-going university reforms will never be achieved and one ambitiously named strategy or programme fails after another – with no consequences whatsoever for those responsible.

So, yes, we can most certainly say that the system is trying to deny the individual the right for self-realization. And it is also true that education is just one of the spheres of life that currently diverges from all those Enlightenment values in which our society allegedly continues to be grounded. But the question is: could this be a structural feature of our society in its present shape, or merely a contingency that has been produced by our lack of awareness, political laziness, trust of 'experts' promoting their own private interest? I would like to believe the latter – in other words, that in principle all these questions can still be solved by the means available to us in contemporary democratic society. And this is where the question of 'applied selfhood', if such a term can be used, again becomes very relevant. 'Self-realization' also entails the process of becoming a social subject, someone able to make informed decisions and political choices.

ZB   There is such a multitude of things we can't control that I can't think of ever making their full inventory. There are always new aporias emerging once we solve one more contradiction among those believed to be hopelessly aporetic. The labour of 'demystifying' the world is likely to go on and on, as cracking of one mystery almost always gives birth to a few new ones; the number of newly spotted unknowns is in fact the most reliable measure of the gravity of the mystery just resolved. The positivist creed that if we've solved one of the 1,000 baffling and haunting problems 999 would've remained to be solved is downright con-tradicted by the story of science and culture in general.

One may or may not agree with Epictetus' advice, but, whatever our stance might be, we would be obliged to admit that the assumed impossibility of a solution hardly ever stopped humans from striving to find it! It seems that, if there is a thing which we better stop worrying about because we cannot control it, the human propensity to go on worrying about things evading control, to stubbornly try to catch them, and to devise ever new and more ingenious nets to do just that, is nevertheless all but ineradicable. History is indeed a long (and far from finished) string of re-classifying as manageable things believed theretofore to be untouchable – such as slavery by Plato or Aristotle or authors of the American Constitution, non-citizenship of women by the writers of electoral laws well into the twentieth century – or, let's hope, hunger being the only stimulus for the hungry to work, while greed being the only stimulus for the greedy to make the hungry work, for the present-day cutters of taxes for the rich and of social assistance to the poor. Or the case you quote, the preor-dained authority and entitlement of business interests expressed in monetary terms to determine the spread and volume of intake of educational institutions as well as the contents of knowledge and kind of skills they offer and impart, as believed by Frans van Vught.

Few people have expressed that simple truth with a clarity more straightforward than J. M. Coetzee, great novelist though also a great philosopher and sublime analyst of the human psyche: 'The runner's sole goal is to get to the front and stay there. The question why life must be likened to a race, or why national economies must race against one another rather than going for a comradely jog together, for the sake of the health, is not raised. A race, a contest: that is the way things are.' (2008: 79). But, he adds, 'There is nothing ineluctable about war. If we want war we can choose war, if we want peace we can equally well choose peace. If we want competition we can choose competition, alternatively we can take the path of comradely collaboration' (2008: 81). Amen.

Where does all that put our problem of the self-production of selves? In the same book Coetzee notes that the concept of sincerity (and so, I would add, of authenticity) is nowadays 'gutted of all meaning'. In the present culture, 'few are capable of distinguishing between sincerity and the performance of sincerity, just as few distinguish between religious faith and religious observance' (2008: 109). Self-realization, presumed to be a DIY job and an inalienable task of the 'self's owner', is, however, much too complex an affair for people trained in the 'nowist' culture (that is, afflicted by a steady shrinking of their attention-span, by shallowing of memory and by fast-growing impatience) to resist the temptation to settle for *performances of self-realization* instead of the real thing. The job of self-producing is considerably, radically eased by the massive supply of mass-produced assembly kits for currently recommended performances – subsequently avidly sought and obtained, with the help of profit-sniffing-and-pursuing mass media and chain shops. I can't help recalling in this context the wit of Vladimir Voinovich, the brilliant satirical writer of the sunset phase of the Soviet Union: with the building of communism in the Soviet Union accomplished by 2042, the communist promise to give everybody according to his or her needs, wrote Voinovich (1988), will have been fulfilled: namely, every day will start with a government radio station announcing what the needs of the population are on that day. The similarity to the practice of fulfilling the promise of the right to self-realization through the supply of kits to represent what currently passes (or ought to pass) for an authentic self, is downright shocking.

What comes to mind as well is Baudrillard's 'simulacrum', in which case the question of its truth or illusion is seeking an answer in vain; or Erving Goffman distinguishing between the ability to do a job well and the skills of convincing the public that the job has been indeed well done, along with his warning about the rising menace of the 'confidence men' mastering the skills of the second kind, though failing or neglecting to acquire and practice the first. Resorting once more to Coetzee's parallel, we may say that what is being nowadays advertised and sold under the label of 'religious faith' is in actual fact the skill of going through (currently ritualized) motions and of employing the paraphernalia serving the public manifestation of its assumed (whether genuine or putative) mastery.

RR Voinovich has simply put in much more colourful terms what Herbert Marcuse actually asserted in his *One-Dimensional Man* as early as 1964: on the one hand, the way the social system works causes problems for the individuals who try at least to preserve, if not realize, themselves within its bounds, but, on the other hand, that same system has monopolized the right to provide solutions to all such problems. And these it can manipulate. Or, as Steven Lukes writes in discussing the views of Bachrach and Baratz, power can most certainly try to influence which phenomena can legitimately be considered problems and which should remain outside the field of justified complaints (2005: 23–5). Marcuse has actually shown how the discourses of instrumentalism, those very same ones that support the idea of 'efficiency above all' in our times, have contributed to the stripping-down of problems of principle to single, individual grievances that can perhaps be taken care of while leaving the system as such intact (1991: 107–14).

In our times, the tendencies since the 1960s have actually even amplified the problem, instead of relieving it (though the development might seem, on the surface, to have been beneficial). It is no longer the case that the system aggressively marginalizes its critics. It grants them the right to their opinion, and a legitimate niche in a multitude of other such subcultural niches, where they can exercise their own choices without upsetting the larger scheme of things. Everyone, even the most radically anti-system protester, has a label derived from what s/he consents to eat and wear. Vegetarians and vegans, boycotters of Nestlé and other environment-unfriendly multinationals, anti-globalists, fur protesters and eco-farmers have all been integrated into the system just as musical subcultures or practitioners of alternative medicine. Spaces which in Marcuse's time made you special precisely because of your decision to step out of the 'mainstream' – and which acquired leverage together with a critical mass of adherents – have now been turned into lifestyle options which are just as mainstream, perhaps even *more* mainstream in certain age and social groups, than their more traditional alternatives.

But maybe we should not be so worried about this? Lukes goes on to describe a 'three-dimensional' model of power, in which the last layer, the usual object of radical criticism, is the capacity of power to shape the beliefs and opinions of those subject to it in a way it likes, so that they genuinely want to do the things their rulers expect them to: 'Power can be deployed to block or impair its subjects' capacity to reason well, not least by instilling and sustaining misleading or illusory ideas of what is "natural" and what sort of life their distinctive "nature" dictates, and, in general, by stunting or blunting their capacity for rational judgment' (2005: 115). This, of course, brings on the basic question of any radical philosophy: who are we to say that these people we are discussing would *actually* prefer to behave differently if this particular power was not blocking their capacity to reason? Why is it that *our* ideas are less misleading and illusory?

I remember a TV show in which Derren Brown, a performer skilled in 'neuro-linguistic programming', was talking to the actor Simon Pegg, asking him to write down on a piece of paper what he wanted for his birthday. After some more conversation, he asked him again what it was, and Pegg answered that his wish would be a GMX bike. And, da-da! – just such a bike was there in the studio. When Pegg then had to read aloud what he had written on the piece of paper previously, however, he was surprised to see that he had hoped to get a leather jacket just a little while ago. Staged for entertainment purposes or not (I prefer to remain moderately sceptical about such wondrous feats), the possibility that our ideas about what is true are not our own is still frighteningly plausible, because such results can, perhaps with a bit more effort, also be achieved by less sophisticated technologies. But if people like Brown have even half the power they claim, then I am sure that quite a few of them are gainfully employed by either great corporations or the powers that be, and constantly trying to get under our skulls.

Thus, it seems we have to ask: how can we actually be so sure that whatever arguments we deploy in the defence of our position against these powers are not themselves also the product of such interference by some other power? In my darker moments, I have sometimes envied the people who manage to live without this basic question bothering them, but, whenever I do, I return to chapter 18 of Voltaire's *Zadig*, in which the protagonist travels in the company of a hermit, an undoubtedly wise man, who nonetheless behaves incomprehensibly – burning down the home of an amiable philosopher with whom they had had a nice conversation the evening before, and killing the nephew of a widow who had offered them her hospitality. All with good reason, the hermit explains to Zadig: the philosopher will find an enormous treasure buried under his house that will make him very rich, and the boy would, in a year, kill his guardian. When Zadig then cries out asking whether, even if someone could foresee the future, it gives them the right to harm a child, the hermit turns from the shape of an ordinary human into that of the angel Jesrad, which, for Zadig, settles the question (Voltaire 2006: 165–7). For me, it doesn't. Which is why I could probably never be a successful politician, let alone a priest or a revolutionary. So, even though I consider a life of self-realization worthier of living than one in pursuit of things other people tell me I should seek, do I actually have the right to impose this view on others?

As Jesrad goes on to tell Zadig, the wicked are always unhappy, and their function is to provide the very small number of good people with ordeals (Voltaire 2006: 167–8), which would, presumably, force their goodness to the surface. Again I cannot agree with the argument, especially with the moral predestination implied by it. Certainly, anyone can choose to live worthily, and there are multiple ways of doing that open before any single person. But, from a slightly different perspective, we can transform it into an argument against laziness and complacency. Do I stubbornly want to pursue my own life as my own, or do I accept a comfortable, ready-made trajectory and go on with it? Can we think about this as a test? Choosing my own path is more difficult, more prone to mistakes – even, perhaps, critical ones. It entails risks the other option has marginalized. But, at least for those who take it, this is the only course leading to satisfaction with one's accomplishments.

This, of course, is not an apology for self-centredness and individualism. What you (and Coetzee) say about collaboration vs competition is tremendously important. Genuine self-realization, I think, can never be accomplished at the expense of others. On the contrary: it is competition that requires everybody to be strong in precisely the same areas. Collaboration makes it possible to develop those areas that are your individual strengths – those where you have something to offer to others. Collaboration can meaningfully only take place between individuals who do not compete with, but complete, each other.

ZB Beware of angels Jesrads, there are throngs of them around, their ranks having grown exponentially since Voltaire's times. To plug one's ears to their siren songs, as Zadig tried in vain to do or rather gave up trying, one needs to be a saint – as Ilya Ehrenburg, in his satirical novel *The Stormy Life of Lasik Roitschwantz* (1960), suggested. In that story, a saintly Tzadik conducting the Day of Atonement prayer was engrossed in his audience with God and about to obtain from God the decision to save the Jews from perdition, when, noticing that Hershele – an old, frail and infirm, untidy and misshapen water-carrier – was about to breathe his last after the day-long fast, he wound up his audience instantly and returned to earth and the synagogue to stop the prayer. Salvation of a whole nation was not worth the loss of old Hershele's life.

In the introduction to their book *The Second Machine Age*, two of the most authoritative spokesmen for cutting-edge technology – Eric Brynjolfsson, the Director of the MIT Center for Digital Business, and Andrew McAfee, the principal research scientist at the same Centre – prognosticate that technology will bring us 'more choice and even freedom' whereby abundance will become a norm, rather than scarcity – noting a few lines further, in passing and with a serene equanimity, that 'technological progress is going to leave behind some people, perhaps even a lot of people', and that 'there's never been a worse time to be a worker with only "ordinary" skills and abilities to offer' (2014: 10–11). Jesrads are today anything but in short supply – it is the saintly Tsadiks and morally (hyper?)sensitive and inquisitive Zadigs who are few and far between.

5

Connected Selves

Rein Raud We have been talking quite a lot about what technology has done to the way people connect to each other in our times. Obviously, as social animals by definition, only very few among us manage to survive without any contact with others of our kind, at least not for very long and without serious damage. But do the ways in which we connect essentially matter? I'd say the internet has replaced god in the twenty-first century, and not in a trivial sense of knowing everything, which it doesn't. A religious person, as far as I have observed, needs to go through her or his religious rituals with some regularity, whether it be just a moment of solitary contemplation or participation in a full ritual, and if deprived of that possibility s/he may develop a feeling of irrational unease, some kind of existential loneliness, a lack of connection to her or his spiritual background system. I feel the same way about the internet. If I haven't had the opportunity to check on my email and Facebook accounts for some time, I feel it increasingly difficult to concentrate on matters at hand – not that I would lose my interest in them, no, but I can't shake off the vague feeling that something is going on behind my back that I have to be a part of, but am not. Especially now when, even if I'm walking in the forest, I can carry a device that connects me to the rest of my world (or frustrates me completely, when, for some technical reason, it doesn't). In his day, Émile Durkheim argued that there is an objective reality in which religious experience is grounded, and 'this reality – which mythologies have represented in so many different forms, but which is the objective, universal and eternal cause of those *sui generis* sensations of which religious experience is made – is society' (1995: 420–1). Religion, according to Durkheim, is thus nothing other than a strangely codified system of paying homage to the fact of being together, and thereby ensuring that this being together can go on without causing too much trouble. 'A faith above all is warmth, life, enthusiasm, enhancement of all mental activity, uplift of the individual above himself', Durkheim says, and then asks: 'Except by reaching outside himself, how could the individual add to the energies he possesses? How could he transcend himself by his own strength? The only hearth at which we can warm ourselves morally is the hearth made by the company of our fellow men' (1995: 427). For the disenchanted Westerner, this hearth is now available in a digital version and with no religious gravy poured over it.

Zygmunt Bauman Your suggestion of a kinship between religious worship and our pious and devout relation to one particular technology that more than any other intruded into, colonized and penetrated (subordinated?) our quotidianity, hits the bull's eye. And quoting Durkheim's 'The only hearth at which we can warm ourselves morally is the hearth made by the company of our fellow men', you flawlessly spot the link between both those variants of 'voluntary servitude' and the thirst for human company.

We – each one of us – live now, intermittently though quite often simultaneously, in two starkly distinct universes: online and offline. The second of the two is frequently dubbed 'the real world', though the question whether such a label fits it better than the first gets more debatable by the day.

The two universes differ sharply – in the worldview they inspire, the skills they require and the behavioural code (order of rites, as you, again rightly, dub it) they conjure up, patch together and promote. Their differences can be, and indeed are, negotiated – but hardly reconciled. It is left to every person commuting between those two universes (and that means to all or almost all, and each or almost each, of us) to resolve the clashes between them and draw the boundaries of applicability of each one of the two disparate and often mutually contradictory codes/liturgies. But the experience derived from one universe cannot but affect the way in which we view the other universe, evaluate it and move through it; there tends to be a constant, legal or illegal but always heavy, border traffic between the two universes.

I suggest to you that one way of narrating the story of the modern era (a way whose pertinence and relevance were made particularly salient by the enthusiastic reception and spectacular, lightning-speed career of informatics technology) is to present it as a chronicle of a war declared on all and any discomfort, inconvenience or displeasure, and of the promise to fight such a war through to the final victory. In that story, the massive migration of souls, if not bodies, from the offline world to the newly discovered online lands can be seen as the latest and most decisive among its numerous departures and developments; after all, the currently on-going battle is being waged in the field of inter-human relations – a territory heretofore most resistant and defiant to all attempts to flatten and smooth its bumpy roads and straighten its twisted passages. The aim of this battle is to cleanse that territory of the traps and ambushes with which it has been notoriously spattered until the advent of online technology. If won, the battle currently being waged may render childishly easy the awkward and unwieldy tasks of tying and breaking human bonds, having liberated them first from the incapacitating burden of long-term commitments and non-negotiable obligations. Many believe, and even more assume matter-of-factly, that the internet is the wonder weapon with which this on-going battle is bound to be, and most certainly will be, won.

The modern war on inconvenience, discomfort, unwelcome surprises and, all in all, on the haunting feeling of uncertainty deriving from the unpredictable caprices of the natural and social worlds, has a long string of antecedents, but it took off in earnest under the impact of the shock caused by the triple catastrophe (an earthquake followed by fire followed by tsunami) that in 1755 destroyed Lisbon, then one of the richest, most admired and proudest centres of European civilization. In the view of the intellectual elite of the time that shock revealed the need to take nature as well as human history under another management – this time guided by human Reason. Two and a half centuries later, Jonathan Franzen suggested in his rightly praised commencement speech at Kenyon College that the 'ultimate goal of technology, the telos of techne' 'is to replace a natural world that's indifferent to our wishes – a world of hurricanes and hardships and breakable hearts, a world of resistance – with a world so responsive to our wishes as to be, effectively, a mere extension of the self'; 'Our technology has become extremely adept at creating products that correspond to our fantasy ideal of erotic relationship, in which the beloved object asks for nothing and gives everything, instantly, and makes us feel all-powerful, and doesn't throw terrible scenes when it's replaced by an even sexier object and is consigned to a drawer' (2011).

In other words: are old dreams now coming true, are the words about to turn flesh? Is the centuries-long war on life's discomforts, thanks to the technology taking the most irksome life troubles off our shoulders, about to be won? Well, the jury (if there is a jury competent to pronounce verdicts) must be yet out. Because there is a price tag attached to successive spoils of war, gains and losses need to be counted – but reason suggests that the balance of gains and losses ought to be calculated *retrospectively*; the time for competent retrospection (let alone for ultimate evaluation) has not, however, arrived as yet.

RR   May I interrupt for a moment to comment a bit on Franzen's words? They make me think of a statement by Simone Weil, whose critique, in 1934, was directed against just the opposite:

> instruments, ceasing to be fashioned according to the structure of the human organism, force the latter, on the contrary, to adapt its movements to their own shape. Thenceforward there is no longer any correspondence between the motions to be carried out and the passions; the mind has to get away from desire and fear and apply itself solely to establishing an exact relationship between the movements imparted to the instruments and the objective aimed at. (2001: 85–6)

Weil's concern seems to be that we, as humans, are forced into shapes that are alien to us, but Franzen is worried that technology now provides us with exactly the things we yearn for. So which is worse? Or perhaps, in the end, they address the same issue from different points of view? On the face of it, Franzen blames technology for giving us precisely what we want to have and Weil blames it for forcing us to be what we are not. But I would argue that the complaint of Franzen is just a version of what Weil says. What if the 'products that correspond to our fantasy ideal' actually correspond to an ideal that is also tacitly forced on us? This time, I am not trapped by the basic question of radical philosophy, because I am speaking for myself: I do not want the ideals the industry expects me to adopt – at least I do not want them voluntarily. If I am, at times or in the end, forced into their mould, this will be the defeat of 'me' as a person. What is replaced is not the actual world with its problems, but my wishes. The result is the same as the one Weil describes: there is no correspondence between my own actual passions and the movements, even the allegedly emotion-laden ones, that I perform. I am deprived of both desire *and* fear, while I need *both* of them to be emotionally whole. And if what I 'want' is immediately given to me, then there is no desire – I can only desire what I cannot have instantly. Desire is a plant, not a seed. It has to grow.

ZB Simone Weil spoke from a society of producers, Franzen speaks from our society of consumers. And so their visions of 'what we are' and 'what we desire' are located in different aspects (sectors?) of the self. They both seem to be accurate – their apparent opposition derives from the difference of contexts, further exacerbated by the 'idealization' of the types they construe. *Homo faber* and *Homo consumens* are both transgressive agents, the 'I am' vision and 'I can make it / I wish it to be / it ought to be' model are separated for both of them and in friction. They are both 'ought driven' – but the transgressive impulse aims in each case in a different direction: at the *world* 'out there' in the case of producers, but 'at *my* self' (at myself) in the case of the consumer. Weil thinks of a producer ceding/losing his creative potential to the machines or expropriated from his/her authorship by the machines, surrendering his/her actions to the impersonal arrangement of Frederic Taylor's working bench or Henry Ford's assembly line: the contraptions whose major purpose was to render emotions and intentions of human 'adjuncts to machines' irrelevant to the results of labour; whereas Franzen speaks of a human surrounded by tempting offers that appeal to emotions of the consuming body, instead of demands aimed at the producer's body as the carrier of labour force. Weil speaks of the human objects of *ex*propriation, Franzen of the human subjects of *a*ppropriation.

We can look at that difference also from a somewhat distinct, albeit connected angle. Considering that both *Homo faber* and *Homo consumens*, all their ideal-typical differences notwithstanding, end up in a similar condition of dependence and a partial loss of autonomy, the conquest and surrender of their selves is attained through application of starkly distinct varieties of power: to borrow terminology from Joseph Nye of Harvard, 'hard' in the case of *Homo faber*, 'soft' in the case of *Homo consumens*. What in the society of producers was pursued and attained mostly with cutting down or eliminating the available options through coercion and enforcement tends to be achieved in our society of consumers mainly with the help of stimulating ever-new desires, temptation and seduction. As Pierre Bourdieu has pointed out in his *Distinction* (2007), by advertising rather than normative regulation.

But allow me to return to one kind of technology – digital informatics – that in my view is currently of the greatest importance to the production of selves. Alain Finkielkraut, a writer/philosopher newly elected to join the small exquisite company of the 'Immortals' of the Académie Française, speaks of the 'malediction' of the internet:

> No doubt, it [internet] offers tremendous services…Researchers, academics, are delighted – they don't have to go to libraries, the journalists can fill their files on invited guests much faster, etc. I however believe that in the universe of communication everything can be said…All the same, it is a world with no faith and no law. It is prohibited to prohibit, as seen on the internet. (*Le Monde* 2014)

Internet: blessing and curse rolled into one and rendered inseparable.

The internet's blessings are many and varied. In addition to the ones Finkielkraut has mentioned by name, let me name as the first and foremost the promise to put paid to one of the most awesome banes of our liquid-modern, thoroughly individualized society, afflicted by an endemic frailty of inter-human bonds: the fear of loneliness, of abandonment, of exclusion. On Facebook, one never again needs to feel alone or dropped, discarded, eliminated – abandoned to stew in his or her own juice and having his or her own self as the only companion. There is always, 24 hours a day and 7 days a week, someone somewhere ready to receive a message and even respond to it or at least acknowledge its receipt. On Twitter, one needs never feel excluded from where things happen and the action is: there are no gatekeepers guarding, and most of the time barring to most people, the entry to the public stage. One does not need to rely on the sparsely apportioned grace and benevolence of TV or radio producers and/or newspaper or glossy-magazine editors. The gate to the public stage seems to stay, invitingly and temptingly, wide open, supplemented with a recorder of visits and 'likes' – that privately owned equivalent of TV ratings, bestseller tables or the tables of box-office returns. Thanks to the internet, everyone has been given a chance of the proverbial 15 minutes of fame – and the occasion to refresh the hope for a public celebrity status. Both appear easy and near-to-hand, as they never did in the past. And the attraction of becoming a celebrity is to have a name and likeness growing more worthy than one's achievement in our world made to the measure of a vanity fair.

These, no doubt, are blessings. Or at least they are deemed, and for good reasons, to be blessings by millions of people sagging and groaning under the burden of abasement and humiliation visited upon them by social degradation or exclusion – or the fear of their coming. Such a gain is huge enough to outweigh the possible losses brought about by the constantly growing number of hours spent online by the constantly growing numbers of the Earth's inhabitants. And let's note that in most cases internet users and addicts are blissfully unaware of what things and qualities they are in danger of losing or what has been lost already – as they had little or no chance of experiencing them personally and growing to value them; today's younger generations were born into a world already split (and since times, for them, immemorial) into its online and offline domains. But what are those losses – recorded or anticipated?

To start with, there are losses afflicting (or suspected to afflict) our mental faculties; first of all, the qualities/capacities thought indispensable to set a site for reason and rationality needed to be deployed and to come into their own: attention, concentration, patience – and their durability. When connection to the internet takes as long as a minute, many of us feel angry about how sluggishly slow our computers are. We are getting used to expecting immediate effects. We desire a world to be more and more like a cup of instant coffee: just mix powder into water and drink your beverage. We are losing patience, but great accomplishments require great patience. One needs to stand up to the obstacles encountered, to the odds which one did not anticipate but that confuse one's projects or dash your hopes of their fulfilment. Much research has been devoted to this issue, and most results show the attention span, capacity for prolonged concentration – together with the virtues of perseverance, endurance and fortitude, those defining marks of patience – all falling, and rapidly. Academic teachers note that their students find it increasingly difficult to read an article (let alone a book) from the beginning to end. An argument demanding consistent attention over more than a few minutes tends to be abandoned well before its conclusion is reached. 'Multitasking' tends nowadays to be the widely preferred strategy in the use of the web with its ever more numerous apps and gadgets, vying for a moment of (even if passing) attention; given the enormity of opportunities, fixing attention to only one screen at a time feels as a reprehensible waste of priceless time.

There are of course indirect yet collateral casualties of such a run of affairs, not yet counted in full and needing more research to evaluate them. Among the best scrutinized, while also potentially most harmful, damages caused by their wilting and the accelerated dispersal of attention are, however, the decay and gradually advancing decrepitude of the willingness to listen and of comprehension powers, as well as of the resolve to 'go to the heart of the matter' (in the online world, we are expected to 'surf' on visually or audially conveyed information; even the until recently popular, but now falling out of use, metaphor of 'swimming' would've suggested something resented for being unduly time-consuming as well as calling for deeper immersion, thereby making progress slower) – which in turn leads to a steady decline in the skills of dialogue, a form of communication vital in the offline world. Closely related to the trends just described is the potential harm to memory, now increasingly transferred and entrusted to servers rather than stored in brains. As the process of thinking (and creative thinking in particular) relies on connections emerging between brain cells, it cannot but suffer from storing information in servers instead. As John Steinbeck is reputed to have said well before the first servers were built in Mojave deserts and cloud internet invented: ideas are like rabbits; you get a couple, learn how to handle them, and pretty soon you have a dozen. We may add: indeed, unless that handling consists in depositing them in warehouses to avoid burdening your own brain.

Next to consider is the likely impact on the very nature of human bonds. Tying and breaking bonds online is immensely easier and less risky than it is offline. Tying them online does not entail long-term obligations, let alone the 'till death do us part, for better or worse'-style commitments, nor does it require so much protracted, toilsome and conscientious labour as offline bonds demand; in case all that proves too complex and onerous and the odds are felt overwhelming, it is easy to withdraw and abandon the effort. Breaking bonds, on the other hand, can be done by pressing some keys and desisting from touching some others, and calls for no awkward negotiation of settlement, nor incurs the risk of Franzen's 'terrible scenes' being thrown. Selecting and reselecting a network of friends and keeping it as long as the heart desires and not a moment longer are achievements attained with little skill, even less effort, and virtually (yes, *virtually*) without risk.

No wonder that, having tested and compared the two kinds of bonds, many internauts, perhaps a large and growing majority of them, prefer the online variety to its offline alternative. Though quite a few others think that those who do so do it to friendship's (not to mention love's) and their own peril and detriment. According to those others, true (that is difficult and risky, calling for constant care and all too often sacrifice) love is the very opposite of its sanitized, play-it-safe electronic quasi-alternative; instead of 'looking forward in the same direction' as Antoine de Saint-Exupéry famously phrased it, the electronic substitute for love is an exercise in bets-hedging focused on defending oneself against the genuine and putative hazards with which design, build and maintenance of a fully fledged love relationship are inevitably replenished. Electronic pursuit of a love relation is guided by the desire for safety, after the pattern of sex with condoms.

One more – perhaps the most contentious – among the issues cropping up in the debate about the blessings and curses of the world-wide web. Universal, easy and convenient exposure to the world's events in 'real time', coupled with opening similarly universal, and equally easy, undisturbed entry to the public stage, has been welcome by numerous observers as a genuine turning point in the brief though eventful and stormy history of modern democracy. Contrary to a quite widespread expectation that the internet would be a great step forward in the history of democracy, involving all of us in shaping the world which we share and replacing the inherited 'pyramid of power' with a 'lateral' politics, evidence accumulates that the internet may serve as well the perpetuation and reinforcement of conflicts and antagonisms while preventing an effective polylogue with a chance of armistice and eventual agreement. Paradoxically, the danger arises from the inclination of most internauts to make the online world a conflict-free zone – though not through negotiating the conflict-generating issues and the conflicts being resolved to mutual satisfaction, but thanks to the removal of the conflicts haunting the offline world from their sight and worry.

Numerous researches have shown that internet-dedicated users can and do spend a great part of their time, or even their whole online life, encountering solely like-minded people. The internet creates an improved version of a 'gated community': unlike its offline equivalent, it does not charge the occupiers an exorbitant rent and does not need armed guards or a sophisticated CCTV network; a simple 'delete' key will suffice. The attraction of all and any – online as well as offline – gated community is that one lives there in the company of strictly pre-selected people, 'people like you', like-minded people – free from the intrusion of strangers whose presence might require awkward negotiation of a mode of cohabitation and present a challenge to your self-assurance that your mode of life is the only proper one, bound to be shared by everybody within your sight and reach. You select people who are mirror reflections of yourself and you are a mirror reflection of them, therefore by living there you are not taking the risk of falling out with your neighbour, of arguing or fighting about political, ideological or indeed any other kind of issues. This is a comfort zone indeed, sound-insulated from the hubbub of diversified and variegated, quarrelsome crowds roaming city streets and workplaces. The snag is that in such an artificially yet artfully disinfected, sanitized online environment one can hardly develop immunity to the toxic controversies endemic to the offline universe; or learn the art of stripping them of their morbid and eventually murderous potential. And because one has failed to learn to do this, the divisions and contentions borne by strangers in city streets appear yet more threatening – and perhaps incurable. Divisions born online are equipped with a self-propelling and self-exacerbating capacity.

Admittedly, the above inventory of actual and potential virtues and vices of splitting the 'lived world' into online and offline universes is far from complete. It is obviously too early to evaluate the summary effects of a watershed-like shift in human condition and cultural history. For now, the assets of the internet and digital informatics as a whole seem to bear a considerable admixture of liabilities – though such an impression could just be reflecting the expectable birth-pangs of new forms of life and the afflictions usually accompanying their maturation. For all that can be asserted at the moment with any measure of confidence, one of the least prepossessing sequels is that of yet higher scores gained by the online universe on the scale of comfort, convenience, risk avoidance and freedom from trouble taking their toll – which by design or by default could prompt/reinforce the tendency to transplant the worldviews and behavioural codes made to the measure of the online life-sphere unto its offline alternative, to which they could be applied only at the cost of much social and ethical damage.

One way or another, the consequences of the online/offline split of the *Lebenswelt* need to be closely monitored.

RR   Let me try to recapitulate a few points you make and compare them to a world without internet. First of all, multitasking. I don't think this is something we necessarily do by choice. More likely, it is required of us by circumstances. A chime of an arriving email interrupts my work on a file just as a doorbell would, and, having dealt with the visitor, I can go back to what I was just doing. A family sitting in front of the TV and quarrelling over who has the remote causes the screen to switch from a sitcom to a football match to a talk show at the very moment the commercial break sets in on whatever channel is currently on, and in the end all the viewers have a certain, though incomplete, impression of the programme they were following. Well, TV is still technology. But consider the traditional housewife. She has food in the oven and potatoes cooking, she constantly watches for signals from the baby as to whether its nappy needs changing, the washing-machine is about to finish its cycle and, in addition, she has to react sympathetically to her older child's story about school bullying. I'd say this is more extreme than most of the stuff we do on the internet, and at least as harmful to mental faculties, simply leaving too little space for their exercise.

Human bonds? In principle, I agree with your point wholeheartedly. I do feel it is always better to communicate with humans directly and not via machines, in particular anonymous ones. But the actual circumstances, especially in a traditional community, may not always have been so desirable either. Breaking offline relationships is indeed very simple and, as I have also remarked earlier, promotes laziness, offers an easy way out of existential problems. Nonetheless, a traditional *Gemeinschaft* (community) and its continuations into contemporary 'team spirit' are not necessarily what I would prefer either: they enforce on every member a mentality that one precisely *cannot* opt out of, a system of values not of one's own choosing, which may occasionally be nice and positive, but can also be dark and oppressive. Suicides by pregnant single girls in religious communities or the emotional dramas of people with divergent sexuality suggest that the possibility of leaving a group is not always an easy – though just about the only – way out. What we would probably both prefer is a balance, a situation where human relationships are symmetrical, formed between equals. This would certainly be my ideal, but in practice this is a rather hard act to accomplish.

Finally, you suggest that the 'internet may serve as well the perpetuation and reinforcement of conflicts and antagonisms while preventing an effective polylogue'. To a certain extent, this is certainly so: militants and extremists can use it as an efficient means to recruit supporters in places they would not have reached before. Trolling and hate speech also proliferate in environments for the much more moderate. But this is not because of the internet; it is because of the people who use it. I agree that the internet has created more possibilities for them to do what they do – however, it has also enabled quite a few with less voice power to speak out and indeed to connect laterally to people with whom it is mutually interesting to disagree. I confess that I spend quite some time on Facebook following and occasionally taking part in political or philosophical discussions, which sometimes get very heated. And it is precisely the point that neither side in these wants to opt out. Most likely, all participants on all sides realize that they will never be able to convince the other fully, but at least they can make the more rational among their opponents see how their arguments work. And sometimes you are surprised by a point made by someone you share most of your views with, but which you could not possibly endorse. So perhaps in the end it works as well as, or possibly better than, say, a debate on abortion between strangers in a pub. If nothing else, then the crowd-sourced selection of information of various origins (quite often from places previously unknown to me) is an asset in itself, something I'd have to spend much more time gathering on my own in any type of library.

To sum up: it doesn't seem to me that it is the internet that is to blame, but the people who use it. We can think of it as yet another Jesrad's test, which offers me the choice between pursuing my own path (and much more efficiently than I could otherwise do) and comfortable, ready-made trajectories into which I can slide without much further ado, accepting the ideals forged for me (in both senses of the word) by cultural industries. Moreover, it is a choice to be made constantly, and I suppose that, just as in other matters of life, we sometimes go one way and sometimes the other. Which is perhaps what being human inescapably entails.

ZB   In Hal Ashby's 1979 film *Being There*, there is a moment when its hero, Chance (played by Peter Sellers), having been evicted from his boss's house in which he spent all his adult life watching the outside world solely on a TV screen, steps for the first time in uncounted years into a busy city street. The first sight he encounters there is a bizarre, never seen before on TV, and therefore baffling and alarming posse of nuns dressed in black. Chance reaches for the TV pilot (forever in his pocket) to efface the shocking picture – presumably to switch channels. He tries, repeatedly and to his utmost confusion, in vain. In the mysterious urban world into which he was exiled, the easy and comfortable ways of getting rid of repulsive and unnerving sights – the ways learned in the many hours spent in front of a TV screen – just didn't work. Chance had indeed a quite serious reason to feel alarmed and confused.

Viewed in retrospect thirty-odd years later, the scene looks like a premonition or a prophetic vision of the dilemmas to come.

Having our life divided between two universes, the online and
offline worlds each with its distinct possibilities and requirements,
and bound as we are to travel daily if not hourly to and fro
between them, we cannot avoid repeatedly bumping into a clash
between the intentions and expectations brought from one universe, and the realities specific to the other: particularly if the first
have been acquired, trained and entrenched online, while the
second were confronted upon return to the offline domain. Well,
the big difference between the case portrayed by solitary Chance
and the case of the millions of contemporary internauts is that
Chance cut a comic and laughable figure, while no one laughs
at the disorientation and embarrassment of those millions of his
descendants.

Remaining inside the online universe, *anyone* can cut out a
'safety zone' – conflict-, unpleasantness- and inconvenience-free;
a secure space, inhabited only by undemanding, like-minded and
therefore non-quarrelsome people – a feat inconceivable in most
working places, on a busy urban street and even on the simplest
and shortest of city strolls. And I repeat: the gravest of the consequences of locking oneself in such a space, a space childishly
easy to construct online yet unattainable – indeed unimaginable
– offline, is a gradual yet unstoppable fading, wilting and decom-
posing of the art of a dialogue: of a genuine dialogue, of a face-
to-face encounter with a different worldview, different hierarchy
of values and different order of priorities – occurrences unavoidable in the offline world, but eminently by-passable online.

And so when you say that it is not the internet that is to blame,
but the people who use it, you are only partly right. People
without internet wouldn't have a similar chance of developing a
taste for staying sheltered from the hazards of 'real life', and while
doing it acquiring distaste for putting their beliefs to the test while
simultaneously losing the will and ability to confront alternative
views, understand them and negotiate a *modus co-vivendi*, agree-
able and beneficial to all involved. And I would add that having
such will and ability, as well as studiously learning and developing
the practical skills needed to act on them, is for our incurably
diversified, diasporized and multi-centred world a matter of
nothing less than a question of life or death.

And I repeat again and again that what I am talking about is
an opportunity created by computer technology, an opportunity

which elsewhere is much less available and handy – not a question of 'technological determinism' (a dangerous fallacy, for all I know and believe in). Not taking up that opportunity is as possible as taking it; obviously, everyone can in principle choose 'political or philosophical discussions, which sometimes get very heated' over the preference for the ego-boosting boon of echo-chambers; and yet with an opportunity to choose the second over the first (a tempting opportunity, given the stubborn querulousness and irascibility of the offline world) made technologically easy to take up and exploit, the probability of such choice is growing.

Technology does not *determine* its human uses, but influences – and heavily – the *distribution of their probabilities*. It makes some choices easier, less costly and thus more likely to be made, while rendering some other choices more difficult to handle and commanding higher prices, and therefore less probable to be commonly chosen. And this is precisely what the research into internauts' practices shows to be happening. And so, while you are absolutely right that we are not and can't be completely stripped of choice and so 'we sometimes go one way and sometimes the other', the odds are that most of us most of the time will plod along the path 'forged (in both senses of the word) by cultural industries' while aided and abetted by computer technology. 'What we would probably both prefer', as in the case of choice between the community and the network variety of human bonds which you discuss, is one thing; the frequency and commonality of actual human choices is another.

And one more point of clarification, which I am making at risk of repeating myself: the problem is not limited to 'militants and extremists [using internet] as an efficient means to recruit supporters in places they would not have reached before'. For such people sealing oneself in a discomfort-free zone would be, as a matter of fact, counterproductive – and only the naïve, sloppy or poorly trained among the canvassers, proselytizers or recruiting officers would resort to such a stratagem. The real problem are the millions tempted and seduced to hide inside the unchallenged and undisturbed tranquillity of echo-chambers and mirror halls by the prospect of ego-boosting, or of better defence of self-esteem, which they slowly but steadily forget how to defend in the hurly-burly offline universe replete with those 'political or philosophical discussions, which sometimes get very heated' – and in which not just political and philosophical discussions get all too often very heated.

RR   But isn't it the case with any technological advancement that it inevitably creates chances for people to do something stupid with it, chances that were not there previously? If the internet is a magnifying glass that can enlarge both wisdom and stupidity to enormous proportions – stupidity being, of course, eminently more visible – can we blame the latter on the instrument? Yes, the internet may well be different from all other similar technological advances in that it provides people with irresistible, or at least previously unseen, temptations, a greater number than ever before. Yes, too many of these people, who could and should do something else, surrender to the call of sirens and emigrate to a world where they have more online than offline time during their waking hours. All that is true, and even more. We know now that pleasurable online activities can even provide for your offline needs, making participation in traditional society less and less obligatory. Even 10 years ago, as Edward Castronova tells us, the national product per capita of the planet Norrath (featured in an online game called Everquest), measured in real money, was about the same as that of Bulgaria (2005: 19). This is because things acquired by performing heroic feats on that planet could be sold to less experienced players for Earth money. So no wonder about 20 per cent of the people playing Everquest, when asked where they lived, responded that they reside in Norrath, although they travel outside quite regularly. About 60 per cent would have liked to spend more time there than they currently did (Castronova 2005: 59). We can imagine this tendency hasn't gone away. So it is not totally impossible that a sizable segment of the Earth's population will in the future consist of zombified bodies, with their minds living elsewhere. Do I endorse this development? Certainly not.

But this raises again the basic question of radical philosophy: on what grounds can I tell these people that they live their lives incorrectly? If they were unhappy and seeking aid, then yes. If they were violent and aggressive towards others, then yes. In the case of alcohol and drug abuse, for example, both of these conditions are usually met. However, as for the internet, it is mostly us intellectuals who tend to admonish people that they are not 'truly' happy online, while the onliners themselves seem to feel as content as they can be, given their realistic alternatives. As to the second condition, the reports emphasizing the crime-prone character of internet addicts are not without their controversies. It is true, of course, that, for example, the Norwegian mass murderer Anders Breivik spent excessive time online before becoming the monster that he is, but in my mind it is incorrect to ask, as Richard Orange does, whether, 'educated by Wikipedia and trained by World of Warcraft', Breivik was, in fact, 'a product of the Internet' (2012). Such a question seems to exonerate Breivik of his crimes to a certain degree: if he was a product of something legally available, then the system is, at least in part, to blame for the deaths of the children he killed, not he himself. I strongly disagree with this. The internet may have provided him with a fertile environment for the development of his insane worldview, but the responsibility for his crimes is his and his alone – in all likelihood, he would have evolved into a dangerous madman in any case, as many other violent fundamentalists have done before him. According to Anne Stickney, the World of Warcraft community currently consists of a little fewer than 8 million subscribers (2014) and a statistically valid connection between the game and excessive violence needs more evidence than just the emotion-driven public outrage over single cases.

So maybe we should treat internet addiction as a symptom rather than the cause of the disease? Perhaps people turn to the internet only as a result of economic, social and cultural problems that they personally cannot handle and nobody else is interested in solving? I remember when, quite a few years back and in another country, I visited a small and depressing provincial town with my son, and after a day, he joked, 'There seem to be only three ways out of this place: the church, booze or the internet.' Of those three, the internet may actually be the least harmful in the long run.

ZB It never occurred to me to 'treat the internet as a *cause* of the disease' (I repeat: for many years now I have staunchly resisted anything remotely reminiscent of technological determinism – whether old-style or 'new and improved') – but I believe that it is more than just a '*symptom* of the disease'. Technology's impact is skewing/contorting/rearranging the probabilities of choices: some choices are made easier and less costly and so more likely to be taken, while some others lose badly in the competition for a

greater comfort, facility and availability, and therefore the likelihood of their being taken is falling. To take up your example: the
causes of your son considering the ways of getting 'out of this
place' are not to be put on the internet's doorsteps – the number
of people joining 'The World of Warcraft' community rather than
a church or the company of booze-addicts would not, however,
rise that high if not for the internet's allure. In other words: at all
times and everywhere, there were, there are, and probably will be
people wishing 'to get away', but, with the internet constantly on
hand, acting on that wish seems to them more safe and less risky
than ever and so becomes easier and more likely to be chosen.
And let me add that the internet wins hands down when competing with church or booze because of its self-boosting power – as
well as the internet-based networks' 'have done it myself', flatter-
ing and self-enhancing 'auctorial' aura (that is, the aura of a
personal union of the author's and the actor's roles), conspicu-
ously missing from the established churches and lost in the stupor
of drunkards' dens.

RR   I suppose it is normal that some people want to get 'away',
anywhere, anytime. But what if the wish to get away is the last
sign that you still have a pulse? All over the world, and not just
in third-world slums, but also in the heartlands of the globalist
civilization, environments are spreading where 'getting away' is
what most people want. Those who can afford it are gone as soon
as they are able to, whatever the strategy. Those who adapt and
internalize the jungle values of these environments will become a
part of the problem that needs solving. The majorities, however,
are trapped. The idea of bringing IT closer to the deprived was
initially, by giving them access to education and information highways, to give them more control over their lives – but, yes, it can
as easily take away what they had. So this is a task left unfinished,
because it has not been thought through.

Perhaps this is where the core of the problem lies. We simply
cannot return to a world without internet, where, among other
things, this dialogue between us would also not be possible. This
is why what we need is a sober relation with it. When paper money
was introduced in Europe, the financial sector did not understand
its nature very clearly and John Law, the Scottish-born French
Controller General of Finances, decided to solve the problems of

the country by issuing quite a lot of such money in order to create necessary resources. What he achieved, in fact, was the plunging of France into economic chaos – which effectually contributed to the advent of the revolution. Again, I would say, the notion of paper money itself was not at fault – rather, the carelessness, greed and limited understanding of the people who used it. Any major technological innovation can cause havoc, unless handled with care and foresight.

So maybe we ought to try to turn Weil's argument around. I still agree with her in principle that technologies that force me to adapt to their normative rules, instead of obeying mine, are not 'friendly' to me – especially when it remains unclear whose interests they serve in the long run. But it can also be said that technological innovations, beginning with the stone axe, have contributed to the evolution of our species precisely because they force us to adapt to them. Weil says that instruments such as the axe are extensions of our body and therefore not opposed to us (2001: 85), but this is not entirely correct. The shape of our hands in their present state is a result of our working with these tools. Our thumbs stand apart from other fingers – and thereby make also quite a few other operations possible, which our nearest relative species cannot handle. Now there are people suffering from a disease called the 'Blackberry Thumb' (Gordon 2008), a severe hand pain caused by prolonged use of the smart phone for typing. Perhaps it is the smart phone that will adapt, perhaps the hand. In any case, body–technology interaction does not proceed without trace. Then why should mind–technology interaction do so? We know what previous technological jumps such as writing, printing and the telegraph have done, not only to our socio-cultural order, but also to the way we perceive things. It had to be expected that a similar change would occur with the internet, the question is how to let it happen without destroying too much of what we hold dear. 'We' here refers not just to people like you and me, but to everyone who would like to preserve the things threatened by the internet, given the choice.

This means that the unfinished task should be taken up again: people should have more control over their world. I suppose there are things that could be done to that end, and even without much trouble – for example, school curricula. Awareness components have often been introduced in various subjects, to create the preconditions of empathy with various kinds of otherness, and there are campaigns for drug awareness, ecological awareness, controlled sexual behaviour. Happily enough, we live in an age where plain telling people what to do is not a functional strategy. But presenting them with reliable analyses of the possible dangers of IT addiction should indeed be a public responsibility.

ZB The 'Blackberry Thumb', by the way, had its predecessors – for instance, the now-forgotten panic of 'Rubik's Cube Palm' in the 1980s – and most certainly it'll have numerous descendants yet. I guess that replacement of quills with pencils and pens, even if left unrecorded, also caused in its time some serious adjustment panics. Such and innumerable comparable incidents of history might be specimens of quite common and quite transient bodily or psychic troubles of re-adjustment and re-positioning, triggered by technology-caused alterations in the field and the setting of action – but such troubles differ considerably from each other when it comes to the width and the depth of rearrangements they require and prompt. And so I don't think that the re-adjustments now on their way can be sensibly compared to those of curing the psycho-somatic afflictions of a 'Blackberry Thumb' or 'Rubik's Cube Palm' kind – marginal, minor and momentary as they quickly proved to be, and soon after forgotten.

The transformation in the human condition and the *Lebenswelt* put on the agenda by the advent of digital informatics and the world-wide web belongs to a not-that-voluminous category of genuine milestones and turning points in the history of the human species, and deserves in that history a chapter fully of its own. This time over, not a thumb or a palm is affected, but the all-embracing, multi-faceted and cumulative complex of life tasks, life strategies, bodily and psychic capacities – all of them together and each one of them on its own fundamental to both the individual and the socially shared existence. I wonder whether any element of human being-in-the-world and any ingredient of the mechanism of human association will ultimately emerge from the current transformation unscathed. Moreover, all those exceedingly numerous and multifarious factors seem to be closely and tightly intertwined – but we are still in a very preliminary stage of unravelling and properly comprehending the nature of their connections and reciprocal influences. And I feel that resorting to the usual call-to-arms of 'people should have more control over their world' stops well short of telling us what needs to be done.

To start with: who are those 'people'? As it happens, some people have evidently too much control over their own world but also over the worlds of others – whereas some other (and by far more numerous) people, as you flawlessly put it, are trapped in places from which exercising any control over anything whatsoever is out of the question. To go on: that 'too much' of the ones and 'none at all' of the others are intimately intertwined – control is, as its very notion suggests, a zero-sum game. For that very reason, each successive settlement of the issue is well-nigh certain to be (in Whitehead's terminology) 'essentially contested' and therefore unstable and probably temporary – binding until further notice, or the nearest major or even minor reshuffle of power divisions and hierarchies. There is hardly ever a shortage of invitations to resistance and revolt aimed at another reshuffling of cards. For all practical intents and purposes, bids for control not yet had, defense of control already attained, and an unstoppable tug-of-war between them are in all likelihood permanent companions of the human predicament.

When all's said and done, control is and will remain the stake and the product of power struggle. The current phase of that power struggle is conducted under the banners of recognition. Erving Goffman has suggested that the ability to compose a specific identity, and the capacity to win recognition that such identity has been indeed composed and that you possess it, are two different skills that may be acquired and mastered separately. Goffman flawlessly recorded such a state of affairs, but, having reduced it to the question of skills mastered by the bidder, he missed the crucial circumstance of the fate having already been tampered with and turned into a loaded die, and odds having been thereby pre-set in a way that renders the appropriation and deployment of skills ineffective. Possession by the bidder of both kinds of skills might be a necessary condition of the bid's success, but it is not its sufficient condition. It is not the bidder – at any rate, not the bidder alone – who decides the success or failure of the bid. Max Frisch has laid bare the division or roles in the 'identification combat', suggesting that the ultimate meaning of 'having identity' is resisting the definitions imposed by others. We have been defined well before our bid is launched, and the building of a self of our choice is conducted on an *a priori* allocated (social) site; it can't be seen through and completed without the approval of local administrators. That rule applies as much to the individual as it does to the collective-selves builders (for instance, to ethnic groups bidding for a nationhood status).

To return to our starting point, I fully agree that, as you suggest, 'presenting [pupils] with reliable analyses of the possible dangers of IT addiction should indeed be a public responsibility'. Choice is the *pupils'* responsibility, whereas responsibility for providing the fullest possible information needed to allow those choices to be made under the condition of maximum awareness of what is involved in the choosing, and what the consequences of various choices are likely to be, is *public*. As I said, I agree. But I would add that, when it comes to considering the contents of a school curriculum that may play a role, however limited, in enhancing the young self-producers' chances of success in their bid for social recognition, the 'road map' tracing the track from chosen identity to its public recognition – complete with natural and social hindrances and traps – needs to be included.

RR To return for a moment to your question, 'who are those "people"?' – which is a very important one indeed. I am still perhaps a bit more comfortable with a Frankfurt-School-style opposition between 'people' and 'the system', a non-coordinated amalgam of business, career politics and infotainment, its values based on the lowest common denominator. Perhaps it is not really some people who have control over the lives of others, even though it is them who look after the needs of the system – they, too, are trapped and cynically successful rather than humanly happy. But for them, too, there is no 'outside', as Michel Foucault has pointed out, even though their inside is fairly comfortable (and what quite a few others desire):

> What makes power hold good, what makes it accepted, is simply the fact that it doesn't only weigh on us as a force that says no, but that it traverses and produces things, it induces pleasure, forms knowledge, produces discourse. It needs to be considered as a productive network which runs through the whole social body, much more than as a negative instance whose function is repression. (Foucault 1980: 119)

We shouldn't, perhaps, include the people on top among the *victims* of this 'system', as it has rewarded them with numerous benefits, but neither are they free or independent agents. So it is perhaps correct to say that those who exercise control are also controlled themselves, just as forms of resistance have long since been accommodated by the system and assigned their own niche, their own chain stores.

I would like to think we can make a distinction between the 'system' and the public sphere, because the public sphere can only function when it is not overruled by the logic of the 'system'. It would, of course, be really sad if this hope for the possibility of the public sphere turned out to be just an illusion contributing to the greater glory of the 'system' in the long run, but I can't help believing in it. The 'system', of course, would like to mask itself as the public sphere, just as tabloids would like us to see them as the voices of public opinion. But these are different things. The public sphere is an Arendtian matrix of power as opposed to a Foucauldian one: the place where power ends when any form of violence begins, brainwashing included. Perhaps it would be correct to say that the 'system' and the public are based on two incompatible logics of connectedness: the 'system's' connections are always vertical – there is always someone in charge and someone on the receiving end – while the public connections are horizontal, with all parties involved empowered equally. I understand, of course, that what is needed is a balance between the two, and a world organized only according to the latter principle would be difficult to inhabit as well, but what we are seeing is that positions of actual power have been taken over by system-thinking people, while public-thinking people are increasingly marginalized, especially when the decision-making mechanisms often manage to convert them, should they be absorbed into them – which, again, makes it possible to represent public-motivated thinking as yet another cynical strategy for getting closer to the rewards of the system.

ZB   While no less than you captivated by Foucault's 'capillary' model of power (as well as by the strikingly akin Gramsci's model of 'hegemonic philosophy' reborn in daily practice of the *hoi polloi*, and the updated version of both: the 'fractality' of power, that is replication of its essential cell structure at every level of the hierarchical order) – I feel all such models need some sort of a rider to avoid the trap of excessive depersonalization of the nature of control. In the final account, it is some people who impose upon some others an order of affairs made to the measure of their own interest and comfort and oblivious or explicitly unfriendly to the interests of others; an order that, rather than 'calling for adjustment', insinuates itself, helped by the endemic sobriety, realism and rationality of sufferers, and by hook and by crook penetrates the mindset and commonsense of the oppressed and settles there.

This reservation acquires particular gravity at the start to the twenty-first century, which – as Thomas Piketty has convincingly argued – may well enter history as the one of the return to oligarchy: 'When the rate of return on capital exceeds the rate of growth of output and income, as it did in the nineteenth century and seems quite likely to do again in the twenty-first, capitalism automatically generates arbitrary and unsustainable inequalities that radically undermine the meritocratic values on which democratic societies are based' (2014: 1). 'Inherited wealth grows faster than output and income...It is almost inevitable that inherited wealth will dominate wealth amassed from a lifetime's labour by a wide margin, and the concentration of capital will attain extremely high levels' (2014: 26). In the result,

> spectacular increase in inequality largely reflects an unprecedented explosion of very elevated incomes from labour, a veritable separation of the top managers of large firms from the rest of the population...Top managers by and large have the power to set their own remuneration, in some cases without limit and in many cases without any clear relation to their industrial productivity. (2014: 24)

Finally, the present-day exorbitantly fast growth of inequality since the Reagan/Thatcher neo-liberal revolution 'is due largely to the political shifts of the past several decades, especially in regard to taxation and finance. The history of inequality is shaped by the way economic, social and political actors view what is just and what is not, as well as by the relative power of these actors and the collective choices that result' (2014: 20).

Not only the right to control but, most importantly, the capacity of controlling – which until not so long ago appeared to have once for all become the stakes in the popular power game called 'democracy' involving the totality of citizens in their capacity as electors – turn nowadays once more into an heirloom of few and far-between families, which it used to be in pre-modern times; also the modern democratic institutions, meant to translate the popular will, and value preferences and the actors' ideas of justice into 'collective choices', have been increasingly recycled into principal vehicles of reproduction, reinforcement and magnifying of the distance between 'the cans' and 'the can-nots', and making autonomous choices has become a privilege of the constantly shrinking category of 'the cans'.

6

The Composition of Selves

Rein Raud When you said that 'we have been defined well before our bid is launched', how much, if any, possible freedom did you credit the individual with? Or is our freedom indeed restricted to selection from available pieces? I've always thought that one of the challenges of being human is precisely to overcome the limits – biological, social, cultural – that the world has imposed on us when we are born. Not to be satisfied with our lot, even though this might not be the most effective recipe for happiness. On the other hand, isn't 'knowing our place' just the way that the system wants us to live? Can that even be done with any dignity?

Zygmunt Bauman I wrote that 'we have been defined... *before* our bid [for the kind of 'self' we would wish to become ours] is launched' – meaning that we never launch such bids from a sort of 'socially pristine void'. We are born in a specific and non-negotiable time and place, but also in a specific social position predetermined by our (un-chosen by us) parentage. This circumstance, by and large, limits the number of our practically feasible/plausible choices. It is easier to reach the set destination from one place than it is from another. To quote an Irish joke: a driver stopped his car to ask a passer-by how to get from there to Dublin – to which the person he'd asked answered: 'if I wished to go to Dublin, I wouldn't start from here'. That joke exposes the inanity of a fact which in real life is anything but hilarious.

I feel uneasy about juxtaposing determination and self-creation, or more generally fixity and freedom, as standing in opposition to each other. These two parameters of the human condition are as much in alliance as they are in conflict. Each of them exercises in the process of self-composition its own potential – enabling as much as disabling. And they are doomed to coexist and collaborate – each being inconceivable, in fact meaningless, without the company of the other.

In my little book on the art of life (Bauman 2008), I argued that life's itinerary is two-dimensional and needs to be plotted on two perpendicular axes: one dimension is what we commonly call 'fate' – the accumulation of factors on which one has no influence, able neither to modify them nor to wish them away. The other is what could be summarily dubbed 'character' – the subjective assets and liabilities one can, in principle, work on (and so for that matter refuse or neglect to work on). Fate may be deemed responsible for the set of options that open invitingly to one actor yet are locked or at least barred to another; it draws a line between realistic and unrealistic options. The actor's character, on the other hand, bears responsibility for the choice among the already fixed assortment of realistic options – while sometimes (though because of the essential rationality of *Homines sapientes*, not very often) prompting a bid (usually, albeit not unexceptionably, vain and unsuccessful) for an unrealistic one. In designing the trajectory of life, those two factors cooperate: laying the whole responsibility for the life's course squarely at the feet of one factor while closing one's eyes to the contribution of the other is grossly misleading. Due to the inescapable interference of two factors, neither of the two creates 'necessities' (as William Pitt Jr put it, bluntly though rightly, in his House of Commons speech given on 18 November 1783: ' "Necessity" is the argument of tyrants and the creed of slaves'). At the utmost, each of the two factors is engaged in *redistributing the probabilities of different choices being made.*

The crucial point is the intertwining of the influences of fate and character in the course of self-composition. Their intertwining is all the more intimate for the distinction between them stops short of overlapping with the opposition between 'external' vs 'internal', 'material' vs 'psychical', and all in all 'objective' vs 'subjective' components or aspects of that composition. Their mutual relation in the course of the life-long labour of self-composition may be compared to that of the warp and weft of a canvass, both woven of the same yarn. After all, fate reaches the actor not only as an alien force, but also (and probably mainly) in the form already processed into a set of adopted and internalized predispositions and preferences (settled firmly in the mindset of the actor, even if – to quote Ernst Bloch – only in an 'anticipatory' or 'not-yet-conscious' form); thinking means venturing *beyond fate*, as Bloch insisted (1995: 4) when distinguishing the 'participatory' reason from its merely 'contemplative' variety, and thereby it trans-steps the status quo. The character, on the other hand, is known to seriously influence the shape and the content of what rebounds on the actor, and tends to be perceived and classified by them as their fate.

The labour of self-composition never ceases; I would suggest that its story could be visualized as a string of present moments, each caught in the act of recycling the future given to the anticipatory, often not-yet-conscious mind, into the past consisting of the traces left behind by the activities of participatory reason.

RR   On the whole, I agree, although my own metaphor would be slightly different: an extension of what is called 'life expectancy at birth'. Normally this expression refers to the number of years one is expected to live. But we could also think of this expectancy more broadly – as of the kind of life one is expected to have in a Borgesian 'garden of forking paths'. We could also draw this out as a tree, with possibilities branching off to the left and right at those innumerable moments when the conditions of one's birth, social and biological, do not determine the choice one makes. But some choices most certainly launch a person on a typifiable stretch of a life-course for a certain period. Some branching points alter the direction of that course irredeemably; other branches lead apart for a time, offering new meeting points higher up. Each of such branching points corresponds to a decision, although we are not always conscious of making them – and to avoid or to delay these decisions may mean only that we delegate them to others.

The influences shaping these decisions are indeed captured very well in the opposing forces of 'fate' and 'character' you speak about. To a point, however, these aspects may also be mutually determining – certain traits of 'character' would be statistically more likely to appear in some 'fate' settings rather than others. But a lot would always still depend on the particular individual. Some people accept their conditions peacefully, others rebel against them. Some rebel against one type of condition, others against different ones. But these rebellions are also moments of choice we face while moving upward on our life-expectancy tree, potentially there from the start.

Obviously, chance and other uncontrollable factors, including what happens on other people's life-expectancy trees, may influence the course of an individual life quite a lot and open up new possibilities altogether, as well as cut off existing ones. But on the whole we could perhaps look at the trajectory of life as something shaped by the life expectancy tree on the one hand and the individual decisions made at each branching point on the other. We create our life as it creates us.

Now if we want to measure the success of a life, one possibility for doing so would be with a yardstick of happiness, perhaps comparing the actual height a person has reached climbing this life-expectancy tree to the height of the tree itself. The problem is, none of the yardsticks we actually use is strictly vertical, and we cannot even see ourselves where this verticality is – or whether it even exists. The yardstick equating happiness with material wealth thus puts the highest point in one place, and the yardstick of, say, spiritual achievement puts it at a quite different point. And neither of these coincides with the yardstick of a harmonious family, or passionate love, or wisdom. All of these are at different angles from each other, which makes them incompatible on the whole, but nonetheless a typical individual would like to do well by at least several of them. So each individual inevitably fails on some counts, while possibly doing well on others.

Of course, such yardsticks of happiness are not our own invention – they cannot be. We make them our own. Still, only a rare, strong individual is able to determine for herself an absolutely rigid verticality by which to measure her progress along her own life-expectancy tree. The majority, I am afraid, go by verticalities that are like reeds at the mercy of socio-cultural winds – sometimes more, sometimes less. And quite often a choice which at the branching moment seems to be the absolutely most correct one to make will later, under different circumstances, be a reason for bitter regret – though, of course, nobody can know what would have really happened in the possible world created by the alternative choice.

What interests me is precisely what takes place at these branching points, and to what extent we are able to make our own decisions there. I quite agree that the 'labour of self-composition never ceases', but neither does the toil of self-production – I'd like to oppose these two terms to each other, 'production' being the work of outside controlling forces for which we are the clay, and 'composition' our own work, where we are the potters – even if, as potters, we have still been previously moulded out of clay. Or perhaps ceramic potters shaping our own clay. What seems to have taken place here over the last few decades is a certain shift that is very well illustrated by the evolution of the popular LEGO construction toys. When I was young and first encountered them, they came in kits out of which you could build your own fantasies, with some inspiring examples presented in the accompanying booklet. By the time my children started to play with them, the concept had changed: each kit was sold with exactly the number of pieces needed to build one certain model, a bit like a puzzle with a correct solution. Of course, if you had many of these, you could still combine them and even remix the different worlds sold to you, but the fact remains that these worlds had become preordained, systematized and internally complete wholes meant for acceptance together with their rules and narratives. Obviously, groups of professional developers can come up with more compelling worlds than a child who has just been introduced to these toys for the first time, so they are winning out in quality hands down. But what they will collaterally have taken away from the child is the necessity to invent these worlds – and the immense joy that comes with it, which is, of course, replaced by the commercially much more rewarding urge to acquire the next piece in the series, the next element of the expanding, but readymade, world. And, predictably, a child who has grown up in readymade LEGO-worlds will have fewer problems in adapting to readymade life worlds as an adult.

ZB I like your 'clay & potter' allegory, and even more your codicil of a ceramic potters (potters' minority) not buying their clay in art shops but setting themselves to prime, groom and knead the clay they mine and use to their own vision/design. This is what

I tried to capture and express when speaking of the internalization of fate by the actor as always involving its selective interpretation; and of 'crude', un-processed fate as always manipulating the actor's chances and predisposition to develop her/his character in this rather than that direction.

I also appreciate your introduction of the 'life's success' issue, which as I guess may be unpacked as the satisfaction derived from 'a job well done': fulfilment of what Jean-Paul Sartre used to dub the 'projet de la vie'. Such satisfaction, a *sui generis* 'meta-happiness', is, however – similarly to other aspects of self-composition – an unstable, flickery sentiment: an ephemeral state, a momentary condition liable to be revoked and even replaced with its opposite. To quote again from Freud: to the question 'what do [people] demand from life and wish to achieve in it?', Freud responds: 'The answer to this can hardly be in doubt ... [People] strive after happiness; they want to become happy and to remain so.' The snag, however, is that they *cannot* 'remain so':

> What we call happiness in the strictest sense comes from the (preferably sudden) satisfaction of needs which have been dammed up to a high degree, and it is from its nature only possible as an episodic phenomenon. When any situation that is desired by the pleasure principle is prolonged, it only produces a feeling of mild contentment. We are so made that we can derive intense enjoyment only from a *contrast*, and very little from *a state of things*. (1991: 264–5, italics added)

As you see, happiness is the very opposite of a 'social fact' which Émile Durkheim postulated as the sole legitimate subject-matter of sociology: a 'thing', marked like all things by solidity, stability, durability and an overwhelming coercive – indeed a hardly resistible, or downright irresistible – power. It is rather the *pursuit* of happiness, and particularly the selection of objects on which that pursuit is targeted and whose appropriation/consumption is expected to be, and consequently tended to be experienced/described as, the moment of happiness, that deserves to be categorized among such 'social facts'.

Let me observe, however, that the natural habitat for pursuing happiness is the state of *un*-happiness, *dis*-satisfaction, *un*-fulfilment – in short the state of pain-generating suffering of deprivation (like being suppressed, alienated, estranged, abandoned, excluded, robbed of dignity and self-esteem, etc., etc.). The above comment could also be put in another way: in the opposition 'unhappiness vs happiness' the first member, unhappiness, is (in the terminology of structural linguistics) 'unmarked'. The second, happiness, is 'marked' – it can be defined solely in negative terms: as the elusive and transient moment of its overcoming, defying, defeating or putting paid to – and all in all its denial...Happiness is the driving force of life pursuits, but, like the rest of the active, guiding, lodestar-type utopias, its 'materiality', indeed its human and social significance, is entirely entailed in stimulating its continuous pursuit and in the durable – though all too often serendipitous (unanticipated, unintended and unplanned) – effects of that pursuit.

Christopher Helman of *Forbes* has reported research conducted by the London based Legatum Institute – one of the many investigations attempting 'to unravel the causes' of human happiness: to find out the quantifiable and codifiable conditions of human happiness. 'Legatum scores the world's countries on entrepreneurship, personal freedom, health, economy, social capital, education, safety & security, and governance', Helman notes. Scores are allocated by *Forbes*' boffins, and *chapeau bas* for the volume of intricate calculations they must have produced in order to arrive to their results, and the volume of energy they had to expend in order to arrive there...Somewhat caustically, Helman comments, however:

Happiness is subjective, not objective, and what defines it can be debated *ad infinitum*. Does prosperity equal happiness? Not always, but it sure helps. Are you happy with your life? Perhaps you've considered that question while stuck in traffic in your fancy car on your commute to your important job in an impressive office building. You've fantasized about jettisoning it all, abandoning the office, the mortgage, the suits, the stress, the 24/7 electronic tether. (Helman 2013)

And so on and on, as the list of the 'subjective' factors defying and casting into doubt the 'objective' ones expands potentially *ad infinitum*.

The Legatum Institute, and numerous other research bureaus, extrapolate from the statistical distribution of responses to questionnaires (though also, and more seminally, from tacit assumptions of the questionnaires' authors concerning 'human nature') to how much happiness people *ought* to have derived from the scores assigned by the researchers to what they assumed were their happiness-producing qualities. But what if some Tom, Dick or Harry has not derived happiness from bearing such qualities? In other words, what if they failed to do what the researchers presumed they should've done? Well, it must be their – Tom's, Dick's or Harry's – error – mustn't it? – or the result of their ineptitude to make good their chances. Because, as the researchers knew before their research started, it is all economy, stupid! Or at least so we, much as did the Legatum boffins, hear daily from people in the limelight.

And again we agree, that human troubles, stumbling, falls and defeats (though, consequently, also the battles won) come in many shapes and colours. The 'feelgood' mood is hardly ever unqualified and complete, whereas the state of unhappiness seldom if ever manages to wipe out its enjoyable moments completely. *Lasciate ogni speranza* engraved at the entry to Hell was no better an anticipation of the trajectory ahead than *Arbeit macht Frei* cast over the gate of Auschwitz.

All that has been said so far bodes ill for the dreamers of a cohesive account of the human predicament, or the cohesiveness of its reality: of straightening up such 'crooked wood as that man is made of', as Kant would say. It bodes ill for the theorists busy with organizing knowledge, as much as it does for the tyrants striving to grasp, hold the pull-strings setting human marionettes in motion. All the same however, all that augurs well for the prospects of the human indomitable and incorrigible pursuit of happiness. And for the immortality of hope.

RR   There is an old joke about a masochist and a sadist, the two sole survivors of a shipwreck, on a desert island: after a while, the masochist walks up to the sadist and asks, 'Would you perhaps like to torture me?' The sadist looks at him, smiles and answers, 'I most definitely will not!'

To try to define happiness in quantifiable parameters, as the Legatum Institute would like to do, is a venture doomed from the start. One person's pleasure is another one's pain. I once actually experienced a tropical island with lots of sun and beautiful people around, the sort of standard image of bliss that Hollywood films have traditionally proliferated. That happened after two months of an intensive and occasionally very difficult expedition through South-East Asia. Our small company got bored by the second day and decided to return to our travelling mode a few days earlier than planned. Standard-issue happiness is like any other standard-issue product: it is supposed to do the trick for the majority, but every single person on Earth certainly belongs to at least one minority – or most likely quite a few – on some count.

And this is precisely why the composition – as opposed to the production – of selves is so important. As a free individual, I have not only the right to the pursuit of happiness, which, along with life and liberty, the United States Declaration of Independence has listed as one of the three unalienable rights of all human beings. I also have the right to commit my own mistakes, provided I am prepared to take the responsibility for them. In fact, I have the right to failures, disappointments, all kinds of troubles – in short, my own unhappiness, again provided I will not impose this condition on others. And obviously I also have the right to follow the trail leading to standard-issue happiness *if I so choose*. However, this is something nobody should force me to do.

Therefore, I am not quite sure whether it is very useful to characterize the state of pursuit of happiness in these negative terms that, together with Freud, you have proposed. After all, there is only a limited amount of stuff that can be learned from other people's mistakes, and a great deal of the satisfaction felt after an achievement is derived precisely from the effort that had been put into the process leading to it. Otherwise newspapers could start publishing already-solved crosswords instead of empty ones. And even if there is a sense of lack underlying the process of 'the pursuit of happiness' – as well as the motivation behind it – there is also the other side to this coin, the all-too-human experience captured neatly by the English expression 'looking forward'. To look forward to something means to take pleasure in that thing already even though it is not yet materially there, not a part of our world physically, but still present in our minds. Yes, sometimes this pleasure may actually be greater than the enjoyment derived from the thing itself. Yes, sometimes the sense of looking forward can actually become the cause for a future disappointment. And it can be misused, manipulated, exploited to cajole an individual into doing something she would not normally decide to do. This is why there also exist hardcore realists – for example, my wife, who denies herself the experience of looking forward, in order not to be deceived by any false hopes. Of course that, too, is her right.

ZB   As you say, 'looking forward' 'can be misused, manipulated, exploited to cajole an individual into doing something she would not normally decide to do'. It *can* be misused? It *is*! Daily, and on a fully and truly massive scale. I would go as far as suggesting that our society of consumers, society deploying the consumerist pattern to arrange and administer all three – personal, group, and societal – of its systemic levels, is grounded in a systematic misuse (or rather abuse) of the 'looking forward' proclivity of its members.

Our society of consumers has managed to redirect that proclivity which Thorstein Veblen 100 years ago traced back to the 'instinct of workmanship' – that is, to an endemic, instinctual desire to do a job well, to derive pride from its perfection, to seek happiness in what Mauro Magatti and Chiara Giaccardi have recently dubbed '*ex*corporation', a propensity and urge to *add* to the world – towards something describable as the 'instinct of consumption', of appropriation and enjoyment of things, of '*in*corporation': the propensity and the urge to *detract* from the world, one by one, the things that have been first trans-substantiated into commodities.

The nightmare for the consumerist economy are precisely those 'hard realists' as your wife, dear Rein: humans who refuse to 'look forward' to new and yet untried enjoyments, who instead opt out of the nearly universal chase after an ever greater volume and intensity of pleasurable sensations; in other words, the '*satisfied* consumers' – people settling for their present level of consumption and deaf to siren voices cajoling or blackmailing them to move on; to voices that denigrate and ridicule or censure the modesty and inertia of the needs/desires/wants for which the prospective clients settled – voices that tempt and seduce those other clients into a state of insatiable thirst for novel and not-yet-experienced objects of desire. And no wonder: satisfied consumers could and would sound a death knell for the society of consumers.

The art of marketing consists nowadays of a twofold strategy of arousing wants for new pleasures and making sure that the happiness derived from enjoying them is maximally brief. The side effect of that strategy is to make the consumerist economy into one of systematic excess and waste. Once it has been capitalized on, commodified and redirected by the consumerist economy, the human, all-too-human inclination to 'look forward' turns all too often to be, as you rightly point out, more pleasurable than 'the thing itself'. Indeed, shopping is *as a rule* more pleasurable than its results – that is, the possession and consumption of the things purchased; in addition, the time-span of its enjoyment, unlike the longevity of the joys of possession, is in principle infinitely expandable – at least the masters of the marketing craft go out of their way to make it so.

You write: 'I am not quite sure whether it is very useful to characterize the state of pursuit of happiness in these negative terms', which I, following Sigmund Freud's observation, propose. I believe, however, that the grounds to characterize that state in such terms have never been as wide and deep, solid and convincing, as they are now, courtesy of our society of consumers. Our society of consumers has developed a powerful, *sine-qua-non* vested interest in reinforcing what is otherwise a universal tendency and forcing the 'characteristic...in negative terms' upon all three levels of the social system – whereas the consumerist worldview hegemonic in this society sees to it that the state of dissatisfaction is kept permanently ready to conceive and propagate ever new visions, models and specimens of happiness-generating objects of desire. It also makes sure that those visions and models do not survive the moment when objects-of-desire turn into things-in-possession.

As I have argued elsewhere, all shops, whichever goods and services they otherwise offer to their customers, draw their power of attraction and seduction from representing themselves (and being perceived, manifestly or latently) as *sui generis* pharmacies – selling medicines against the afflictions caused by the rat race and a hurried life, pains and anxieties generated by existential uncertainty, moral scruples inflicted by the frailty of inter-human relations, and, all in all, shameful and humiliating 'under-performance' in the art of life – manifested as it is in the irreducible distance separating 'getting forward' from the 'looking forward'. And as we know only too well, the financial security and profitability of the pharmaceutical industry grow together with the number of sufferers seeking a remedy for their torments among the drugs piled on their warehouse shelves. For more drugs to be sold and at greater profit, that industry needs more, not fewer illnesses – and more, not fewer life conditions defined and believed to be pathological, that is as calling for treatment and essentially curable. Whether genuine or putative, the sheer availability of a drug recycles wants into obligations.

RR With all of what you are saying about the contemporary consumer society, I fully agree. What I do not think, however, is that this society has managed to irrevocably institutionalize the entire spectre of the human condition. As I was saying earlier, Marcuse in the early 1960s had already pointed much of this out: it is in the character of the 'system' to create unreal, illusory needs for people, which it then purports to satisfy. Nonetheless, the 1960s saw a massive upheaval against the system, both in the West and parts of the Eastern bloc. The pendulum has now swung again to the opposite end, and many of the ideals of the 1960s are no longer credible, but I sincerely do not believe this means that the human condition is done for. It is true that for most of us there is no alternative to being complicit with the system to a certain degree. Even the eco-farms providing chemically uncontaminated products to the more enlightened (and richer) customer have become a part of the system and occasionally sell their stuff through the same supermarket chains. Eco-tourism is advertised through websites. In that sense, there is no going back. So what needs to be achieved is a *modus vivendi* – or, if necessary, a take-over. There must be ways for the parts of the system that we cannot do without to be used to create new spaces and oases within the system for those who are not satisfied with the standard issue. And this is already happening. Crowd-sourcing is a good example: financing start-ups or cultural projects that prefer to stay out of the reach of the big corporations, that are reaching their prospective audiences directly, which gives a chance to niche products and endeavours that would have died at the crazy-idea stage just a few decades ago. Small and practically non-profit publishing houses have carved out for themselves a significant bit of quality territory in the literary market. Even in mainstream popular culture, the producers who used to proliferate aggressive myths have slowly been forced to adjust their ideologies and listen to independent critical outlets such as Anita Sarkeesian's 'Feminist

Frequency' videoblog. And so on. I am not suggesting that the current situation is fine, simply that all is not lost.

However, what I had in mind with 'looking forward' as a necessary part of our self-composition was actually something other than looking forward to future enjoyment during consumption, even though the consumerist machine would no doubt very much like to hijack the meaning of these words. I may just as well be looking forward to a long walk in the park. But what if it rains? Or the visit of an old friend. But what if we quarrel, as we sometimes do? If we tie our pursuit of happiness to an idea of perfection, we will never achieve anything, because rain and quarrels are and have to remain a part of our lives just like sunshine and harmonious friendship. This is so often forgotten. That, too, is at least in part an effect of consumerism: all of us have only limited resources of time and money at our disposal, so one way to measure our achievement is to find out whether we have used them most efficiently – whether we walk in the park only on sunny days and every party we throw is a 100 per cent success. In other words, the degree of perfection we have managed to reach.

There is nothing wrong with striving for perfection, but once perfection has been defined, it becomes a problem – because movement stops. In that sense, perfection is death, because in death, too, there is no change. So we can perhaps conceive of perfection in two different ways: as a final destination, the end point of a given track, the realization of the dream we have been looking forward to – or something that cannot be measured by absolute and immutable standards, and always evades us as the gray dot between black squares in the famous optical illusion. And that can obviously be used to keep alive the desire for something new – something better as well: a desire neatly captured by a *graffito* I once noticed on a wall in Berlin: *Alles wird besser. Nichts wird gut* (Everything becomes better. Nothing becomes good).

These two opposite attitudes towards perfection are, in fact, quite well illustrated by the differences in Western and Japanese aesthetics. In the West, arts have always been a little closer to the sciences than in some other parts of the world in that the idea of a 'correct' artistic representation is not alien to them. For example, even though scholars such as Erwin Panofsky (1991) and Nelson Goodman (1968) have convincingly demonstrated that geometrical perspective is not the correct or even the most natural way of depicting a three-dimensional world in two-dimensional space, the conviction is still widespread that this artistic convention is a proper, scientifically grounded way to depict reality. So, while on the one hand Western arts give due credit to the artist's individuality, they simultaneously imply the existence of rules, within which creative perfection must be realized. Of course, no cultural practice can do without any rules, and this is true of Asian arts as well. Nonetheless, the attitude towards them is different. The very character of these rules is different.

We spoke before about emulation as one possible paradigm of self-performance. Aesthetic perfection can similarly be approached through emulation. The Japanese word *kata* indicates the proper way to do anything – for example, to prepare or even to eat some complicated food, or to draw one's sword from its scabbard, and some people train for years in order to achieve perfection in some such practice. But someone who has achieved *kata* is not imprisoned by it. On the contrary – once the model has been internalized to the degree that it can be emulated without conscious effort, one is free to do as one pleases. Rules no longer apply. The master can err against the simplest regulations that a beginner must strictly abide by – because a master only does that with good reason; and because no rules are absolute as laws of nature would be, but only the safest bet, the easiest way to navigate the constant flux. What the attainment of *kata* teaches is not perfection, but its ultimate absence. It is not, cannot be a matter of degree, things cannot be more perfect or less perfect. Which is why a handmade tea bowl which may even have (something that looks like) a visible defect is always preferable to a faultless factory product that does not differ from others of its kind. It is the same with lives.

ZB You propose to invest hopes in, for instance, 'financing start-ups or cultural projects that prefer to stay out of the reach of the big corporations'. The snag is that most of those start-ups and projects manage 'to stay out of range' only as long as they live from hand to mouth, struggling day in, day out, to survive. The first big hit, though, is in most cases sufficient for one or another of the 'big corporations' to tempt them into a 'friendly' or force into an unashamedly hostile merger ('merger' being a politically correct codename for a big fish feasting on one that is smaller but tasty – a codename used by the corporate beasts of prey and the pipers they paid when setting their tunes), followed by a routine asset-stripping (politically correct name for burglary) and staff redundancies. Indeed, their lack of success (that is, un-expanding demand and absence of profit) is the very condition of the small, local, toddling initiatives' survival. In our market-misruled world, the price of autonomy is insignificance. One can, alas, be pretty sure that if the 'start-ups or cultural projects', or indeed the small uncompetitive publishing houses you have in mind, are left alone and bypassed by corporate predators, this happens because their prospects of success are in the predators' opinion minimal or nil. More often than not, the pioneering, groundwork labours done by the 'crowd-sourced', noble individuals' or groups of enthusiasts' initiatives, prove retrospectively to have been an unpaid, voluntary work of laying out new meadows for corporate grazing; or reconnaissance sallies to explore and map new territories for a successive corporate expansion.

Resistance against such a sad turn of events is of course possible, and the instances of a gallant and occasionally durable 'against-all-odds' defence being attempted are ample; this hardly, however, adds stability to the permanently touch-and-go, frail and 'until further notice' existence. Once the corporate forces are free to exercise intermittently their awesome 'hard' and 'soft' powers of enforcement, bribery or seduction, the odds against survival are overwhelming. If in doubt, recall the sorry fate of the noble idea of 'kibbutzim', or the half-enforced but half-voluntary, often enthusiastic, surrender of the British non-profit 'mutual societies' to the greed and rapacity of the banks.

As to your unpacking of the intentions behind the idea of 'forward looking': it shows that what you had in mind was a blend of determination strong enough to withstand unfavourable, and thus discouraging, odds, with readiness to settle for results short of perfection. And so you advise against the two sins of the feebleness of stamina and intolerance of pedantry: on that point, there is no disagreement between us. But when reacting to your discussion of 'forward looking', what I had in mind was Ernst Bloch's concept of 'living-towards-future', in his view the ultimate truth of the human condition (the authentic in man and in the world, as Bloch penned down, is their potential: waiting, living in fear of being frustrated and in hope of succeeding). It is the 'forward looking' proclivity in this Blochian sense that in my view has nowadays been intercepted, seized, conquered and colonized; and it is just such proclivity that continues to be capitalized on by the consumerist markets in the daily practice endorsed and legitimized by the life philosophy hegemonic among the denizens of our society of consumers.

I also fully agree with you on the undesirability (but also unattainability) of the 'state of perfection', famously defined by Leon Battista Alberti as a state in which any further change is bound to be for the worse. Assumption of the perfectionist attitude signals/inspires an unwholesome mixture of intolerance, insensitivity and moral blindness. Once believed to be known in advance, 'state of perfection' is prone to legitimize and exonerate most inhuman, lethal, callous and merciless 'the goal justifies the means' practices. Albert Camus has said that much, when he averred that the distinctive trait of the modern kind of evil is being committed in the name of the most lofty and noble ideas. Camus is also known to opine that the real generosity towards the future lies in giving all to the present.

Striving for perfection in the second of its two meanings – of the drive to make things (the objects of action, or the acting skills of actors) better than they have been thus far, the effort of 'perfecting' resting on the belief in the endless 'perfectibility' of things, rather than an effort to reach 'perfection' based on a belief that, since entities differ in their degree of goodness, one of them must be 'perfect', that is, better than any other conceivable alternative (a reasoning deployed by Saint Anselm in his proof of God's existence) – can be seen, however, as a commendable endeavour: indeed, a fly-wheel of continuous change, self-reflection and criticism. Fortunately, such striving is also an inseparable companion of the human mode of being-in the world, even if (regretfully) alongside its opposite: the tendency to routinization.

Let me, however, say on this occasion a few words from Jeremy Rifkin's most recent book (2014), in my view very relevant to our concerns and discussion. The answers Rifkin offers to your (but also my) attempt to spot a light at the end of the tunnel through which we stumble presently – answers grounded in an admittedly large volume of facts – combine into a radical challenge to the prevailing creed of our times, expressed and embraced from the top to the bottom of society: from the sophisticated philosophy of the learned classes down to the commonsense of the *hoi polloi*.

What Rifkin argues is that an alternative to capitalist markets, widely albeit wrongly viewed as an eternal feature of human nature, is not just conceivable, but already born and gaining ground – likely to become dominant in a matter of not centuries, but a few decades.

To put Rifkin's thesis in a nutshell, capitalism is on the way out, gradually yet unstoppably and irreversibly replaced by 'collaborative commons': an apparently new mode of cohabitation, though one deeply rooted in pre-capitalist history. Commons predate, as Rifkin reminds us, the modern/capitalist institutions and are in fact 'the oldest form of institutionalised, self-managed activity in the world' (2014: 16). And to explain in a shortest possible way how the starting point and the point of arrival of the current transformation differ: 'While the capitalist market is based on self-interest and driven by material gain, the social Commons is motivated by collaborative interests and driven by a deep desire to connect with others and share. If the former promotes property rights, *caveat emptor*, and the search for autonomy, the latter advances open-source innovation, transparency, and the search for community' (2014: 18).

By that capitalism which he considers to be currently on its wane, Rifkin means 'a unique and peculiar form of enterprise in which the workforce is stripped of its ownership of the tools it uses to create the products, and the investors who own the enterprises are stripped of their power to control and manage their businesses' (2014: 43). Whereas the 'collaborative commons', Rifkin insists, are not a utopian fairytale of a never-neverland, but a reality around the next corner; a reality separated from the present condition not by a revolution, world war or another catastrophe, but by an 'exponentially shrinking' stretch of time needed by the already-planted, budding and flowering forms of togetherness and modes of communication, that are procuring energy and resolving logistical problems to reach maturity. Rifkin suggests that the 'contemporary commons' can already be seen. They are composed by 'billions of people' who engage in the deeply social aspects of life. They are 'made up of literally millions of self-managed, mostly democratically run organizations, including charities, religious bodies, arts and cultural groups, educational foundations, amateur sports clubs, producer and consumer cooperatives, credit unions, health-care organizations, advocacy groups, condominium associations, and a near endless list of other formal and informal institutions that generate the social capital of society'. We may conclude that the social capital needed by the 'collaborative commons' to ascend is already in place and amplifying, waiting to be harvested, garnered, set to work. Once fully mature, collaborative commons will 'break the monopoly hold of giant, vertically integrated companies operating in capitalist markets by enabling peer production in laterally scaled continental and global networks at near zero marginal cost' (2014: 23).

I believe Rifkin to be right when he calls us to rip off the curtain hung by the market-run consumerist society to hide increasingly tangible and realistic possibilities of alternatives to itself, of a society of *collaboration* instead of *competition*. Here, however, my agreement with Rifkin grinds to a halt. Calling us – rightly – to resist the temptation to neglect or dismiss the however inchoate sprouts of commons-style social settings (all majorities cannot but begin from a tiny minority, and the most branchy of oak trees originated from tiny acorns) is one thing; quite another is a doubtful – to say the least – suggestion that the case for the collaborative commons replacing capitalist markets is by now open-and-shut and the outcome of current transformation is predetermined... This smacks of a new version of 'technological determinism'. But axes can be equally easily used to chop wood or heads – and while technology determines the set of options open to humans, it does not determine which one of the options will eventually be taken and which suppressed. The route of technological development is not a one-way street, and even less is it a street pre-designed and laid out in advance of its construction. While the question of 'what the humans *can* do' can and should be addressed to technology, the question of 'what humans *will* do' is, however, better addressed to politics, sociology, psychology – with the trustworthy ultimate answers likely to be obtained from them only with the benefit of hindsight.

RR   But Rifkin is speaking about the same tendency that I referred to, isn't he? So the danger of being taken over by corporate sharks, if successful, should be imminent for the commons as well? I agree that the 'have a cigar' story, to borrow the phrase from Pink Floyd – the almost trivial trajectory of talented young musicians achieving some success and then giving in to the temptation offered by

a big label and absorbed into the mainstream – can equally well
be applied to start-ups or any other 'self-managed, mostly democratically run organizations, including charities, religious bodies,
arts and cultural groups, educational foundations, amateur sports
clubs, producer and consumer cooperatives, credit unions' and so
on, if they prove to be viable and possibly start to threaten the
position of some giant operating in the same field. The question
is precisely 'What will humans do?', but I believe that, for many,
the experience of an egalitarian, idea-driven collective does not let
one be sucked up easily into a hierarchically organized army of
suits. More often, such people move on to creating something new.
And here, at least, they have the liquidity of the social structures
of the present world to thank for that possibility. Put briefly, even
though I wish the collaborative commons success in all fields, I do
not believe they have the capacity to oust capitalistic structures
from their entrenched position – but what they certainly can do
is provide a lot of people (and, primarily, successful people with
innovative potential) with organizational experience that gives
precedence to the free spirit over corporate logic, without too
much regard for the material benefits a surrender to the latter
might bring along.

But let us get back to the issue at hand. David Levine has
recently formulated the precondition of a free individual as 'the
potential to live a life not yet determined' (2013: 92), which for
him means first and foremost not determined by greed. Or, we
might add, by prescriptive trajectories of what one must have, be
and do at any given stage of life – or by an urge to become
someone else, someone conforming better to the norms and ideals
imposed by the socio-cultural environment. 'A life not yet determined' is what fits a self not produced, but composing itself – and
by composing, I hope you agree with me, we are not thinking of
someone arranging ready-made elements into a pleasing assem-
blage, but something akin to the work of a composer. Music, too,
can only emerge from sounds that are perceptible to the human
ear – that is, sounds that are, in a way, already there, as words of
a language or colours on the palette. But phrases can be both old
and new. A traveller in a foreign country can get by in most situations using only ready-made phrases, conversation scripts that
you find in a phrasebook, and we all enact such small-talk sce-
narios in countless settings on a daily basis. There is nothing

wrong with this, as such language keeps communication channels open and establishes contact between people, opening up for them a common ground. What is wrong, however, is being reduced to such language, encapsulated by it. And the same, I believe, applies to all other spheres of activity: there has to be music in all of them, and by music I mean not the mechanical reproduction of a piece by a novice piano student, but an unpredictable, yet harmonious co-improvisation by accomplished musicians playing together, always as if for the first time, collaborating towards a process that defines each of them as individuals and all of them as an *ad hoc* collectivity. This is something we all are at any given moment.

Afterword – ZB

Introducing the central theme of our electronic conversation, namely the essential instability of conditions under which selves are nowadays composed, reproduced, preserved, abandoned or lost, we referred to the wider phenomenon of 'non-equilibrium' or 'dissipative' systems, described in much detail by Ilya Prigogine – especially in *Exploring Complexity* (Nicolis and Prigogine 1989). As a simple example of such a system, whose state is frail and subject to abrupt and irreversible change, Prigogine asks us to imagine a pencil in a vertical position, balanced on its tip: the slightest lateral force would cause a fall from which that 'system' would never recover on its own. Full technical description of such system needs specialist terminology that Prigogine supplies; in it, arguably the most crucial roles are played by the concepts of perturbation and turbulence. When transplanted to the semantic field of self-building, re-building and, for that matter, dissipation, they would go a long way towards explaining the observed fragility of selves and the awesomeness of the task of their preservation in our endemically turbulent liquid-modern setting.

Throughout most of our electronic exchanges we tackled the issue of the 'self' as such, and its 'production' as such, concentrating on the features all selves and all cases of their production share, and only occasionally mentioning their (the selves') diversities. But 'selves' come in many shapes and colours, and so do the settings, mechanisms, procedures of their production – and indeed the very likelihood of their production being undertaken, pursued and seen through by the 'auctors' presumed and expected to perform that task. Our portrayal of the intricacies of self-production would be grossly incomplete were we not to attempt to restore in our account a proper balance between uniformity and diversity in the overall picture – lest it escapes the attention of eventual readers of our conversation and distorts the message it should have been in our intention to convey. That diversity is primarily brought about and sustained by the differences in the volume of perturbations and the degree of turbulence to which various categories of population are likely to be exposed. That volume and that degree vary considerably as we pass from one sector of the social structure to another. Let me now therefore try to survey, however briefly, that heretofore neglected side of the phenomenon which we try to dissect and reconstruct in all its aspects.

I believe that an excellent point from which to start has been offered by Joseph Stiglitz and Göran Therborn in their out-standing, trail-blazing and stage-setting contributions to the recently resurrected and currently on-going public debate on social inequality, its devastating impacts and the frailty of prospects for its cure or even mitigation. The picture painted by Stiglitz is best conveyed by a concise, but hologram-like, statement: 'We have empty homes and homeless people' (2013: xli). As the complex canvas is inch by inch unravelled, what we come to see are 'huge un-met needs' confronting 'vast under-utilised resources' – idle workers and idle machines, both cast out of service by the chronically and systemically malfunctioning markets. Alongside unstoppably rising inequality, fairness and the sense of fair play (2013: xlvii) also fall collateral victims to that inanity. Victims of inequality are not only those on the receiving end of economic, healthcare, educational and, all in all, *social* discrimination: as numerous social studies document, it affects the quality of life of the society as a whole. They show that the volume and intensity of most social pathologies correlate with the degree of inequality (as measured by the Gini coefficient) rather than with the average standard of living as measured by income per head. But, of course, people crowded in the lower regions of the wealth-and-income hierarchy are hit most severely – and in all aspects of their life's quality. As Therborn puts it: 'Inequality always means excluding some people from something. To be poor means that you do not have sufficient resources to participate (fully) in the everyday life of the bulk of your fellow citizens.' For the poor, even more than for those immediately above them, 'the social space for human development is carved up and restricted' (2013: 21–2). Therborn considers as the most correct of all on offer Amartya Sen's definition (1992) of the norm which the state of inequality violates: the norm of 'equality of capability to function fully as a human being' – which means the capability of exercising what a given society in a given time considers to be an inalienable human right. And he goes along with Martha Nussbaum (2011), pointing out that the rights which inequality violates or, for all practical intents and purposes, denies and bars (alongside survival and health) are 'freedom and knowledge (education) to choose one's life path, and resources to pursue it' (Therborn 2013: 41). Obviously, we can add therefore to that list of violated or denied rights *the right to self-production, self-assertion and the resources indispensable to pursuing them.*

The ranks of individuals, as well as groups or categories of individuals, whose human rights so understood have been in practice seriously eroded or even expropriated altogether are steadily expanding; the number of those who manage to escape unscathed the effects of market tremors and turbulences are steadily shrinking. To a case study of these interconnected tendencies currently in operation, Stiglitz dedicates a chapter entitled 'America's 1 Per Cent Problem' (a phrase picked up soon after by the 'Wall-Street occupiers'). He found out that the number of citizens who, despite the credit crash, 'managed to hang on to a huge piece of the national income', was confined to but 1 per cent of the US population (2013: 2). Such a concentration of income at the very peak of the economic pyramid hierarchy was not, however, a novelty brought about by the recent economic catastrophe: 'By 2007, the year *before* the crisis, the top 0.1 percent of America's households had an income that was 220 times larger than the average of the bottom 90 percent. Wealth was even more unequally distributed than income, with the wealthiest 1 percent owning more than a third of the nation's wealth.' The disproportion is probably still on the rise and acquiring more impetus, as, just before the banking collapse, between 2002 and 2007, 'the top 1 percent seized more than 65 percent of the gain in total national income', whereas 'most Americans were actually growing worse-off' (2013: 2–3).

The average pay of corporation 'Chief Executive Officers' has become more than 200 times greater than that of a typical worker (2013: 26). And all of these are, let's note, statistical *averages*, failing to expose fully the extremes of person-to-person distances and their expansion.

One of the most salient and probably the most seminal impacts of the impetuous growth and the profound transformation in dimensions of inequality is the sharp differentiation in the degree of human autonomy and realistic opportunities for self-definition and self-assertion – indeed, of the chances and capabilities of self-production allotted and available to individuals placed on different levels of the wealth-and-income hierarchy.

Let's be clear about it: the idea of self-production was the invention, battle-cry and practice of middle classes, awkwardly positioned as they were between the upper classes who *needed to do nothing* in order to maintain their position guaranteed to them by birth, and the lower classes who *could do nothing* to improve the positional constraints imposed on them by birth. 'Middle classes' belonged to the only sector of society (but one that was growing and hoped – as well as still hoping – to grow yet more), to which the postulate of 'meritocracy' (i.e., social rewards faithfully reflecting the value of the individual's contribution) was addressed and tested in practice. It was widely expected that, thanks to the entrenchment of the democratic mode of human coexistence, the 'middle classes' would go on expanding at the expense of both – the top and the bottom – extremes of the social pyramid; and that the postulate of meritocracy would therefore spawn equal opportunities for well-nigh the whole of society – putting paid to class divisions and providing an effective tranquillizer for the conflicts of class and for class antagonisms (remember the vision of the on-going 'embourgeoisement' of the working class, a hard-core element of the 1960s social-scientific commonsense?). Now, however, the middle classes are conspicuous primarily by the fast and apparently unstoppable shrinking of their ranks, together with their trademark trust in the (by now all but ethereal) promises of the meritocratic creed and their hopes for a favourable turn of fortune. The present-day middle classes watch, haplessly and helplessly, the capabilities of self-creation and self-assertion being levelled down, not up, and degrading them to the fixity of fate previously reserved for the lowest strata of the social hierarchy.

Guy Standing has coined the term 'precariat' to denote the new predicament and the emerging mode of life and mindset of the categories of people not so long ago classified as members of the 'middle classes' (2011). That term refers to the endemic precariousness (instability, fitfulness, capriciousness and, all in all, vulnerability) of existence: a condition that several dozens of years ago was deemed to be a particular, class-defined bane of the 'proletariat'. Now the middle classes, in droves, are pushed and pulled to savour the bitter taste of that condition of which Lyndon Johnson, when launching his project of the 'Great Society', famously opined that a man cast into it is not – and can't be – free. Here, 'not free' means, first and foremost: stripped of capability to self-create, to choose, to shape and to control one's mode of life. We are all, or most of us, 'middle class' now – but not the sort of middle class which abbé Sieyès had in mind when, almost two and a half centuries ago, he boisterously and proudly declared the 'third estate' destined 'to be everything', called to make itself such, as well as being capable of successful fulfilment of that calling.

'The prospects of a good education for the children of poor and middle-income families' are 'far bleaker than those of the children of the rich'; 'Parental income is becoming increasingly important, as the costs of college tuition increase far faster than incomes'; 'As those in the middle and at the bottom struggle to make a living...families have to make compromises, and among them is less investment in their children' (Stiglitz 2013: 118–19). In other words, just as in the case of the Hebrew slaves in ancient Egypt, who were told to go on producing as many bricks as before though without the straw previously supplied by the pharaoh's agents, the offspring of the middle- and low-income families are told to go on self-producing as they did before, though this time without the tools which such production requires.

And so, goodbye to the dreams of meritocracy; *lasciate ogni speranza*, you, who enter a world in which, in Stiglitz' summary, 'we are not using one of our most valuable assets – our people – in the most productive way possible' (2013: 117). In other words, when the bulk of those entering are booked to the debit, not to the credit, of that world. And when up to half of new entrants are forced to accept jobs (in the case they are lucky enough to find any) far below their ambitions, talents and skills, and offering little or no security, let alone a chance of self-assertion. And when they watch a steadily growing number of their elders, who seem to have thus far managed to compose respectable and gratifying selves, now in their fifties find their hard-won and laboriously composed identities denied, their hard-won and cherished position in society withdrawn, and themselves relegated to the categories of the redundant and of social liabilities. And let us recall that Dante chose the inscription 'lasciate ogni speranza, voi ch'entrate' to be engraved, as its trade-mark, on the entry gate to Hell.

We can learn much about the probable outcomes of that profound change from the results of the recent elections to the European Parliament. Those elections, unlike the elections to national parliaments, are believed to have little if any practical impact on the conditions under which the electors expect to conduct their life struggles in the foreseeable, let alone a more distant, future. They serve the electors instead as a sort of safety valve: occasions to let off the explosion-prone excess of steam, to vent the blood-poisoning grievances and get rid for a time of potentially toxic emotions – and all that in a relatively safe, because innocuous and inconsequential, direction. The most salient mark of the last European Parliamentary election was an unprecedented proportion of electors deploying that opportunity in full and coming to the polling booths in order for no other purpose except shouting 'Woe!', 'Good Heavens!' – and 'Help!': such pleas having been notably deprived of a specific addressee defined in currently established political terms. As Timothy Garton Ash summed it up in a recent issue of the *Guardian*:

> So what were Europeans telling their leaders? The general message was perfectly summed up by the cartoonist Chappatte, who drew a group of protesters holding up a placard shouting 'Unhappy' – and one of their number shouting through a megaphone into the ballot box. There are 28 member states and 28 varieties of Unhappy. Some of the successful protest parties really are on the far-right: in Hungary, for example, Jobbik got three seats and more than 14% of the vote. Most, like Britain's victorious Ukip, draw voters from right and left, feeding on sentiments such as 'we want our country back' and 'too many foreigners, too few jobs'. But in Greece, the big protest vote went to the leftwing, anti-austerity Syriza. (2014)

This is why I believe the lessons of these elections to be especially illuminating for the theme of our conversation. Unhappiness was indeed, it seems, what prompted citizens of Europe to vote (note that, for the first time in EU history, the number of voters did not fall), even if the assumed/putative culprits of their unhappiness differed from one country to another. For all one can guess, few of the people coming to express their unhappiness and vent their wrath in public trusted any of the people on the list of candidates to be able to alleviate their misery, and any of the competing programmes of sanitation to be effective. Unlike in the case of national elections, when electors must be careful to keep out the candidates whom they see as portending an even worse plight than others for their foreseeable future, the elections to the European Parliament, viewed by most electors as a hopelessly impotent institution, offered an opportunity to express the wholesale frustration safely and risk-free. What moved a great number of the electors was an ambient 'frustration fatigue', the dashing of hopes that (as Peter Drucker had warned already a few decades ago) salvation would ever come 'from on high'.

The protest against the direction in which things are currently going, the most vociferous message of these elections, was not directed against any particular section of the extant political spectrum – but at politics in its present shape, usurped as it is, or is widely believed to be, by the elites who are increasingly aloof and distant from the problems which, most of the time, occupy and absorb most of the energy of 'ordinary people'. That politics as a whole is seen by many as nearing bankruptcy – no longer able to assure the regular supply of the straw needed to make the bricks.

Neal Lawson, the head of 'Compass' (an organization introducing itself on its web page, www.compassonline.org.uk, as 'building a Good Society; one that is much more equal, sustainable and democratic than the society we are living in now'), and one of the most insightful and inventive minds on the British political stage, interprets the results of the European elections as a clarion call to vindicate the citizens' right to a 'citizen-led politics of everyday democracy, not just a vote once every five years'. 'The election result', he suggests,

> makes the case for a new politics overwhelming. The future can neither be denied nor avoided. The world is changing – we either bend it to us, to build a good society, or we will be forced to bend to it. Which way it goes depends on our ability to change and on

how good we are at politics – our wit, wisdom, insight, good faith
and perseverance. Now more than ever, we cannot say we weren't
warned.

To this, he adds words of encouragement: 'at the very time the
old politics is disintegrating, new ways of being and doing are
opening up that give us hope' (2014).

If there was a common denominator to the unhappiness manifested by the otherwise starkly disparate categories of Europeans,
it was – or so at least it seems to me – by the practical, if not
explicit, expropriation of politics from the citizens whom it was
meant and designed to serve and by whom it was meant and
designed to be made. But, as Abraham Lincoln proposed and
insisted a long time ago, no man is good enough to govern another
man without the other's consent. Self-production, self-composition
and self-assertion are not only some among many inalienable
human rights, but also the building blocks of the 'citizen-led everyday democracy' which Lawson had in mind.

Mauro Magatti and Chiara Giaccardi, the two professors of the
Università Cattolica del Sacro Cuore in Milan briefly referred to
before, published several weeks ago a fundamental study under a
challenging title, *Generativi di tutto il mondo unitevi!* (2014). The
subtitle defines their oeuvre as a 'Manifesto of a society of freedom'.
In the centre of the authors' attention are (to express it in my own
idiom) the chances and the prospect of the 're-subjectification of
work', or of restoration to workers of the status of subjects (or of
'auctors' – personal unions of authors and actors) of which they
were expropriated in the course of modern history. It is in order
to denominate the product of the reunification of the actor's and
author's roles that Magatti and Giaccardi coined a new concept
of 'generativo'. The semantic gist of that concept is perhaps best
conveyed in English as 'creative individual'.

Magatti and Giaccardi neither suggest turning back the clock
of history nor demand retreat from the modern individualization
that, as well as introducing new threats to the self, opens after all
new horizons for individual contributions to the material and
spiritual wealth of the human *Lebenswelt*. To act generatively,
they write, means to decide the value and to make it flesh. That
value is precisely the enrichment of the world we share, not its
impoverishment, as in the hunter's-style, privatized utopia. The

logic of 'generativity' is at cross-purposes with the logic of consumerism. It is not guided by the will to '*in*corporation' (that is,
appropriation of things and, by the same token, withdrawing them
from circulation and shared use and enjoyment), but by the intention and practice of '*ex*corporation': 'Generativity is a mode of
life whose purpose is assisting others in their being, care of their
life and volume of their life resources. Freedom of individual self-
assertion, if combined with the generative personality, is capable
of multiplying the material and spiritual affluence of the human
world, and with it – and thanks to it – also the meaningfulness
and moral quality of human existence and coexistence. Such a
combination, if we succeed in the effort to substitute it for the
present-day mode of self-creation and self-assertion based as they
are on rivalry instead of collaboration, has a chance of preventing
the demotion of humanity to the level of a zero-sum game. Freedom
of individual self-definition united with the practice of 'excorpora-
tion' is a warrant for growing richness and diversity of human
potential – but also for enhancing the space for self-definition and
self-constitution of all of us and each of us. Solidarity of fate and
endeavours derived from and supported by generativity won't
stand in opposition to the purpose of individual self-assertion;
quite the opposite, it would become its best – the most loyal and
reliable – ally. Such solidarity is, in fact, a necessary condition of,
and the best warrant for, its success.

Solidarity is ever alive, even if it is all too often suppressed into
near-invisibility by modern social settings aimed – by design or by
default – at de-skilling people in the arts it requires. It is a possibility ingrained in the genetically engraved sociality of our human
species. I fully agree with Richard Sennett, when, following
Amartya Sen and Martha Nussbaum, he points out that 'human
beings are capable of doing more than schools, workplaces, civil
organizations and political regimes allow for...People's capacities
for cooperation are far greater and more complex than institutions
allow them to be' (2013: 19).

Afterword – RR

Now, at the end of our discussions, I feel somehow compelled to return to the beginning, if only to find out how my own view of the problems has evolved as their result. And it undoubtedly has. Reasons of space will not permit me to recapitulate all the topics we have touched, so I will revisit only a few, which have been for me particularly significant.

The issues around selfhood have always had a special importance for me for two reasons. On the one hand, I come from a strongly individualistic culture, and a historical context in which the right to that culture was rudely suppressed during my youth. This is possibly the reason why I have always thought that individual freedom is a necessary precondition for any kind of collective freedom, and any idea of collective freedom that denies this is actually the opposite of what it purports to be. Individual freedom, in turn, implies that the person in question has maximal control over the particular range of life choices available to her or him. 'Maximal' does not mean 'unlimited', of course, but with this caveat the principle itself is something I would consider a universal basic right of every human being, even though it is rarely realized in a satisfactory manner. How the extent of that control over one's own life is determined is thus one very good way to approach the problem of selfhood.

On the other hand, my studies of cultural history and comparative philosophy have shown me that there is no such thing as a universal, 'hard-wired' selfhood-defining structure within us. We are, of course, all born with inclinations to become one sort of person or another, but the context in which our initial genetically programmed potentials are realized and transformed into something else is always social and cultural. The structural principles, or ways in which selfhood comes into being, are not something shared by all cultural and historical settings, and they change over time. How they are changing in the present has, of course, been one of our central concerns.

But when we look closely, we can feel a certain tension, if not a downright contradiction, between these two positions. If there is no uniform, biologically determined selfhood-generating mechanism all of us are endowed with at birth, how then can we speak about a universal principle of individual freedom? Who precisely is to have maximal control over her life choices? The answers to these questions – and consequences drawn from them – are wildly different depending on whether we are speaking about a Cartesian, undivided, self-identical *cogito*-based subject, or, for example, a Buddhist 'no-self', a temporary relation between consciousness-producing elements that have come together in an unstable, shifting alliance. And yet, I think, we have managed to find a common ground where these extremes, as well as many different positions, can be discussed at the same time: the idea of selfhood as an on-going *process*, a lived practice, something we do rather than are.

From this standpoint, the question of how the self emerges acquires additional overtones. A process is necessarily open and does not take place of itself, on solely its own terms. In that sense, we should look for selfhood not strictly within the confines of a biological human body, but, as Andy Clark has suggested (1997: 213–14), also include what it has at its disposal in the immediate environment, its 'peripheral devices', so to speak. A part of my memory is what I have stored in my brain. But another part of it extends to what I have written down in my notebooks and files, or in the margins of books I have read and that are in my library, and obviously of course on photos taken of me or by me and stored in my albums – just as my glasses and my false teeth are a part of me in the process of my interaction with the physical world. I would take that even further: there is a common experience of remembering certain things at certain spots on one's fixed trajectories, at a certain intersection of city streets, or near a particular tree in the forest, where a heated argument has taken place or a solution to a difficult problem has first taken shape. In that sense, the processes of our selfhood are even partially spread out in the physical environment. On the other hand, taken as a lived process, our selves are constantly reshaped also in our interaction with our significant others: when we speak and do (or don't do) things that do not correspond *exactly* to the desires and repulsions of our consciousness at that very moment, we can say we have an internal tension between our urges and our behaviour, but it is important to note that this tension is *internal*, a part of the process of self, and not an opposition between the thing within and the tamed outside appearance – or the tamer who has brought about the latter. In any case, the borders of a self are much more vague than the received view of Western philosophy might have us believe.

And this is something that, in our times, is constantly confirmed by our social and cultural practice, which is why a large part of this book has also been preoccupied by the question of what technology can do and does to the human condition, now that we cannot consider it to be a separately existing phenomenon, but something that has, for good, established itself in the territory of our selfhood. But more than any of our traditional 'peripherals', contemporary information technology, in particular, can affect our relations with the social order and the powers behind it. I remember very well how, just a couple of decades ago, the internet was celebrated as the ultimate tool for spreading democracy and helping people to emancipate themselves from their unsatisfactory circumstances, and to a large extent it has indeed contributed to these processes. Social networks, as uncontrolled channels of spreading information, have played an important role in recent revolutions and power struggles, and mostly on the side of the oppressed. Totalitarian and traditionalist regimes are investing a lot in Great Firewalls, but luckily enough these can still be penetrated, and complete radio silence has become impossible to maintain. In the West, costly and risky enterprises of publishing independent ideas have become much less costly and risky, when this is done online. People, whose immediate socio-cultural environment may be hostile to them for whatever reason, are now able to connect and interact. Accordingly, nobody needs to dread existential solitude any more.

All of that has happened, and more. But not only that. Just like any other technology in history, IT will serve the goals of those who use it, and these goals have never been unambiguous. The more powerful a technology, the better it can be used to control and dominate. Looking back at our discussions from this perspective, I see that both of us have alternated between two positions here, that is, been guilty of something that Bruno Latour accuses modern thought of: appealing to two incompatible views at the same time, and choosing whichever argument is better for the given moment (1993: 35–7). When discussing phenomena of the contemporary situation we don't like, one of us has laid the blame on the technology, or the system, and the other has countered this by saying that it is not the instrument or institution that is to blame, but the people who use it for their own selfish ends. And yet both of us would then resort to an argument similar to the other's, from another perspective, a few pages later.

I think this is an issue that needs clarifying, not least because it relates directly to the central questions of selfhood: how much control does each of us have over the process – and accordingly, how great is our individual responsibility for its outcomes, in particular the effects of our own acts on the lives of others? How can we claim the glory for our achievements if we blame the circumstances when anything goes wrong? Do we think what *we* think or what we are conditioned to think? And finally something that I call the basic question of radical philosophy: how is it possible to believe that other people would have made different (from our point of view, more correct) life choices, if they had been free of those particular influences that shaped them? How can we tell that *our* ideas about life are better than theirs?

I do not think anyone will ever be able to solve these issues for good, so all I can do is to offer a particular perspective. First of all, let us consider the process of enculturation. Quite clearly most of what we know is not invented by ourselves, but learned, so having ideas created by others is not necessarily a bad thing in itself. On the other hand, quite a lot of what our parents and teachers transmit to us with love and the best of intentions proves later to be invalid, if not downright harmful to us, at least from our own perspective of that later moment. This, too, is natural, and means the world is alive and changing. Things we learn when young may well lose what I call 'cognitive adequacy', or the capacity to provide us with satisfactory and satisfying (though not necessarily correct) answers to questions about our life world. In addition to that, all cultures without exception have values that can be used to justify and generate harm, and this does not always go unnoticed by the people, especially if the harm is directed against their own interests (or what they consider to be such). We may not be born with the proverbial 'bullshit filters' that help us distinguish information that works for us from what does not, but the inevitable contradictions between our life world and received views about it force us to develop them sooner or later. So at certain moments it is normal that the knowledge we have acquired in the process of growing up seems inadequate to us, even if it is not, in itself, always malicious. However, a certain part of it is, and those who want to seduce or indoctrinate us most certainly want to bypass any barriers we try to erect to protect us, and make us believe it is our own thoughts, or at best reflections of objective reality that they are mediating to us, not ideas that are supposed to work for them within us. Given the extent of their effort, I'd say it is inevitable that they succeed to a certain degree. For example, it seems the political parties that openly defend the interests of the rich in many countries get quite a lot of the vote from the poor – because, first, the poor have internalized the view that the division of society into the rich and the poor is inevitable, and secondly, because they want to become rich themselves as well, and they start by behaving politically as members of the group they would like to belong to.

But, to rephrase our original question: who is this 'they'? For the answer, I think, we might look at the development path of institutions and organizations. A new firm, for example, can begin as a start-up with very democratic organizational culture, something that Tom Burns and G. M. Stalker have classically called an 'organic' system (1994), which is also good for the development of innovative ideas and practices. Nobody has strictly defined responsibilities and no one would ever refuse a task because it is not in her or his job description. On the other hand, neither is anybody authorized to give others tasks they do not consider meaningful. At a certain moment, however, such organizations often grow too big to be managed that way and, to use Burns' and Stalker's terms again, a 'mechanistic' system of routinized procedures with strictly defined responsibilities takes the place of the slightly chaotic self-regulation. This usually happens when the number of people is too big for everyone to know each other – in other words, when a degree of alienation is reached. The arrival of such a moment is only logical, it is structurally built into the matrix of growth – after all, it is normal for us to relate differently to people with whom we live and work side by side and to those to whom we are bound by evanescent institutional ties only. However, it seems to me, this is also the moment when the 'interests of the organization', distinct from the sum total of the members' interests, are born. The institution, no longer the fruit of the connection between people, but the agent connecting them, acquires its own life-logic and its own goals. These are at the same time the extension of the interests of its members, but also of the factors suppressing them – although the balance between the two is obviously different at the top and at the bottom. Over time, the interests of the institution – be it a corporation or a country – tend to crystallize around a core, which makes it difficult for later leaders to change directions completely, and tempting for anyone who has reached that position to sit back and enjoy. Organizations are not unlike technology in that they can both be adapted for personal use and require adaptation from persons – not only their members, but just about anyone who gets into contact with them. And, obviously, just like any living organism, an organization wants to survive and flourish, which in turn requires attention to material gains. And once these start to determine your course of action, there is no turning back.

Above, I have defined what could be called 'the system', in the tradition of the Frankfurt School, as the non-coordinated amalgam of business, career politics and infotainment, its values based on the lowest common denominator, or money and the pleasures of consumption it contains as a potential. In a Foucauldian way, we could say that 'the system' is not to be found anywhere, but manifests itself as 'natural' behaviour expected of certain social positions as well as discourses of efficiency and economic performance as universal ways of measuring the value of things. From the present perspective, 'the system' is the next step, the organization of organizations, and thus doubly the product of alienation. Inequality is one of its necessary conditions not only because it needs to concentrate material resources into the hands of a few, but also because it needs poverty as a state of mind, it needs the poor who desire to become rich, to marry the princess and to get a half of the kingdom. 'The system', let it be said – just in case – should not be confused with the public sphere, which, contrary to its opposite number, is looking for the highest common factor to base human interaction on: a space in which it would be possible for every individual to remain themselves, just not at the expense of others.

Obviously, 'the system' as defined here also has a strong interest in participating in the production of selves, and has lots of resources at its disposal to that end. I would still be inclined to think, however, that technology has always been merely one of these resources and not a danger in itself. Innumerable losses of life and treasures have occurred throughout history because of fire, and yet the taming of fire has been a necessary condition for the human species to evolve into what it is. Any powerful technology needs to be used with great care. Such care should certainly be a part of our socio-cultural competence, and its development a public responsibility. Nonetheless, when we speak about the 'interests of the system', these are still derived from human interests, despite all the alienation (which itself is originally a part of the human self-defence arsenal, a by-product of the need to be left alone). Man-made tools, at least until the hypothetical advent of techno-logical singularity, do not have any such independent interests of their own. However, this does not make them any the less danger-ous if they are used to cause you harm. But if those tools are used to create circumstances for you to harm yourself? This is where the matter becomes tricky. One of the fathers of liberalism, Ludwig von Mises, in 1927 famously argued that all hard drugs, including cocaine and morphine, should be commercially available in spite of their harmful nature, because the state, or the majority of citi-zens, should not in principle have the right to impose any restric-tions on what the individual could or should consume (2005: 31). Today, I suppose even the staunchest of liberals in actual politics would not be likely to advocate such a position. Still, I would side with the liberals concerning the present issue in that public aware-ness is surely a more efficient tool to help those in need of guidance to steer clear from dangers they, all things considered, would themselves like to avoid. But we cannot impose our preferred world on those gamers who want to emigrate to the online planet of Norrath of their own free will and who consider that to be the

optimal life choice available to them – at least not until they
declare war on our planet in some manner or other. The deplorably narrow range of the life choices available to many is another
problem entirely, and a very serious one indeed.

So where does all that leave us, regarding the initial questions?
It has never been easy to be human, nor should it be, and each
age has its own new challenges. This is the way it has always been,
and on the whole our present age – with its tools for realizing
creative human potential, combined with hitherto unseen social
mobility – is much to be preferred to most other time-spaces,
where even discussions such as this would not have been thinka-
ble. I would also say that it is the challenges of our present world
that have enabled us to formulate the basic questions about selfhood much more accurately and precisely than has previously
been possible. Needless to say, such questions will never receive a
final, unalterable answer, and this is how it should be.

Perhaps it is fitting to finish with two moments of wisdom from
the opposite ends of the world. First, a story about the Chinese
Chan master Ruiyan of the Tang dynasty (618–907), from the
'Checkpoint Without Gates'. Every morning, it is said, Ruiyan
woke up and called himself: 'Master!' And then answered himself:
'Yes, sir.' Then he told himself: 'Sober up!' 'Yes, sir.' 'And do not
let other people deceive you again!' 'Yes, sir, yes, sir!'

And finally, the words of Archipoeta (1130?–1165?) who, nine
centuries ago, so beautifully captured a feeling many of us today
know only too well:

> *Cum sit enim proprium*
> *viro sapienti*
> *supra petram ponere*
> *sedem fundamenti*
> *stultus ego comparor*
> *fluvio labenti*
> *sub eodem aere*
> *nunquam permanenti.*

(While it would be more appropriate for a wise man to base
his seat on a fundament of stone, stupid me would rather
be compared to the flowing river, never the same under the
unchanging sky.)

References

Alexander, Jeffrey C. 2006. 'Cultural Pragmatics: Social Performance between Ritual and Strategy'. In *Social Performance: Symbolic Action, Cultural Pragmatics, and Ritual*, Cambridge Cultural Social Studies, edited by Jeffrey C. Alexander, Bernhard Giesen and Jason L. Mast. Cambridge University Press.

Ash, Timothy Garton. 2014. 'Europe: The Continent for Every Type of Unhappy'. *The Guardian*, 26 May.

Barthes, Roland. 1990. *The Fashion System*. Berkeley: University of California Press.

Bauman, Zygmunt. 1988. *Freedom*. Milton Keynes: Open University Press.

Bauman, Zygmunt. 1991. *Modernity and Ambivalence*. Cambridge: Polity.

Bauman, Zygmunt. 2000. *Postmodern Ethics*. Oxford: Wiley-Blackwell.

Bauman, Zygmunt. 2005. *Liquid Life*. Cambridge: Polity.

Bauman, Zygmunt. 2008. *The Art of Life*. Cambridge: Polity.

Bernstein, Eduard. 1993. *The Preconditions of Socialism*. Cambridge University Press.

Bieber, Matt. 2013. 'Online Exclusive: Interview with Todd May'. *Believer*, 11(4).

Bloch, Ernst. 1995. *The Principle of Hope*. Cambridge, Mass.: MIT Press.

Blow, Charles M. 2014a. 'Accommodating Divisiveness'. *New York Times*, 22 February.

Blow, Charles M. 2014b. 'Minimum Wage, Maximum Outrage'. *New York Times*, 16 April.

Boltanski, Luc, and Eve Chiapello. 2007. *The New Spirit of Capitalism.* London: Verso.

Borges, Jorge Luis. 1999. *Selected Non-Fictions.* New York and London: Viking.

Bourdieu, Pierre. 1993. *The Field of Cultural Production: Essays on Art and Literature.* Cambridge: Polity.

Bourdieu, Pierre. 2007. *Distinction: A Social Critique of the Judgement of Taste.* Cambridge, Mass.: Harvard University Press.

Brodsky, Joseph. 1995. *On Grief and Reason.* New York: Farrar, Straus & Giroux.

Brynjolfsson, Erik, and Andrew McAfee. 2014. *The Second Machine Age: Work, Progress, and Prosperity in a Time of Brilliant Technologies.* New York: W. W. Norton & Co.

Burns, Tom, and G. M. Stalker. 1994. *The Management of Innovation.* Oxford University Press.

Carlin, George. 2001. *Napalm & Silly Putty.* New York: Hyperion.

Castronova, Edward. 2005. *Synthetic Worlds: The Business and Culture of Online Games.* University of Chicago Press.

Clark, Andy. 1997. *Being There: Putting Brain, Body, and World Together Again.* Cambridge, Mass.: MIT Press.

Coetzee, J. M. 2008. *Diary of a Bad Year.* London: Vintage.

Cohen, Daniel. 1999. *Nos temps modernes.* Paris: Éditions Flammarion.

Collins, Nick. 2013. 'Hawking: "In the Future Brains Could Be Separated from the Body"'. *Telegraph*, 20 September.

Crozier, Michel. 1964. *The Bureaucratic Phenomenon.* London: Tavistock Press.

Derrida, Jacques. 1997. *Of Grammatology.* Baltimore and London: Johns Hopkins University Press.

Descartes, René. 1991. *The Philosophical Writings of Descartes.* Vol. III, *The Correspondence*, translated and edited by John Cottingham, Robert Stoothoff, Dugald Murdoch and Anthony Kenny. Cambridge University Press.

Durkheim, Émile. 1995. *The Elementary Forms of Religious Life.* New York and London: Free Press.

Ehrenburg, Ilya. 1960. *The Stormy Life of Lasik Roitschwantz.* New York: Polyglot Library.

Foucault, Michel. 1980 *Power/Knowledge: Selected Interviews and Other Writings 1972–1977*, edited by Colin Gordon. New York: Pantheon Books.

Franzen, Jonathan. 2011. 'Technology Provides an Alternative to Love'. *The New York Times*, 28 May.

Freud, Sigmund. 1991. *Civilization, Society and Religion*, edited by Albert Dickson. Harmondsworth: Penguin.

Gadamer, Hans-Georg. 2004. *Truth and Method*. London and New York: Continuum.

Goffman, Erving. 1990. *The Presentation of Self in Everyday Life*. New York: Anchor Books.

Goodman, Nelson. 1968. *Languages of Art: An Approach to a Theory of Symbols*. Indianapolis: Bobbs-Merrill.

Gordon, Serena. 2008. 'Beware the "Blackberry Thumb"'. *The Washington Post*, 15 June.

Helman, Christopher. 2013. 'The World's Happiest (And Saddest) Countries, 2013'. *Forbes* (October).

Kaufmann, Jean-Claude. 2012. *Love Online*. Cambridge: Polity.

Kay, Paul, and Willet Kempton. 1984. 'What Is the Sapir–Whorf Hypothesis?' *American Anthropologist* 86: 65–79.

Latour, Bruno. 1993. *We Have Never Been Modern*. Cambridge, Mass.: Harvard University Press.

Lawson, Neal. 2014. 'Post-Election Statement: Leaving the 20th Century'. London: Compass.

Le Monde. 2014. 'Alain Finkielkraut s'emporte contre la «malédiction d'Internet»'. *Le Monde*, 10 April.

Leach, Edmund. 1964. 'Anthropological Aspects of Language: Animal Categories and Verbal Abuse'. In *New Directions in the Study of Language*, edited by Eric H. Lenneberg. University of Chicago Press.

Leach, Edmund. 1966. *Rethinking Anthropology*. London: Athlone Press.

Leach, Edmund. 1971. 'Language and Anthropology'. In *Linguistics at Large*, edited by Noel Minnis. London: Gollancz.

Levine, David P. 2013. *Pathology of the Capitalist Spirit: An Essay on Greed, Hope, and Loss*. New York: Palgrave Macmillan.

Lotman, Yuri M. 1992. *Izbrannye Stat'i*, Vol. I. Tallinn: Aleksandra.

Lukes, Steven. 2005. *Power: A Radical View*. 2nd edn. Basingstoke, New York: Palgrave Macmillan.

Magatti, Mauro, and Chiara Giaccardi. 2014. *Generativi di tutto il mondo, unitevi! Manifesto per la società dei liberi*. Milan: Feltrinelli.

Marcuse, Herbert. 1991. *One-Dimensional Man: Studies in the Ideology of Advanced Industrial Society*. Boston: Beacon Press.

May, Todd. 2009. *Death*. Stocksfield: Acumen.

Mead, George Herbert. 1972. *Mind, Self & Society*. 18th edn. University of Chicago Press.

Nicolis, Grégoire, and Ilya Prigogine. 1989. *Exploring Complexity: An Introduction*. New York: W. H. Freeman & Co.

Nussbaum, Martha. 2011. *Creating Capabilities: The Human Development Approach*. Cambridge, Mass.: Belknap Press.

Orange, Richard. 2012. 'Norway Killer Breivik: A Product of the Internet?' *GlobalPost*, 19 April.

Panofsky, Erwin. 1991. *Perspective as Symbolic Form*. New York: Zone Books.

Pascal, Blaise. 1966. *Pensées*, translated by A. J. Krailsheimer. Penguin Books.

Pascal, Blaise. 2003. *Pensées*. New York: Courier Dover Publications.

Pessoa, Fernando. 1991. *The Book of Disquiet*, edited by Maria José de Lancastre. London: Serpent's Tail.

Piketty, Thomas. 2014. *Capital in the Twenty-First Century*. Cambridge, Mass.: Belknap Press.

Plath, David W. 1980. *Long Engagements: Maturity in Modern Japan*. Stanford University Press.

Prigogine, Ilya. 1997. *The End of Certainty: Time, Chaos, and the New Laws of Nature*. New York: The Free Press.

Prigogine, Ilya. 2003. *Is Future Given?* New Jersey and London: World Scientific.

Rifkin, Jeremy. 2014. *The Zero Marginal Cost Society*. New York: Palgrave Macmillan.

Schleiermacher, Friedrich. 1998. *Hermeneutics and Criticism*. Cambridge University Press.

Sen, Amartya. 1992. *Inequality Reexamined*. Cambridge, Mass.: Harvard University Press.

Sennett, Richard. 2011. *The Foreigner: Two Essays on Exile*. London: Notting Hill Editions.

Sennett, Richard. 2013. *Together: The Rituals, Pleasures and Politics of Co-Operation*. London: Penguin.

Simmel, Georg. 1950. *The Sociology of Georg Simmel*. New York: Free Press.

Sperber, Dan, and Deirdre Wilson. 1998. 'The Mapping between the Mental and the Public Lexicon'. In *Language and Thought: Interdisciplinary Themes*, edited by Peter Carruthers and Jill Boucher. Cambridge University Press.

Spivak, Gayatri C. 1988. 'Can the Subaltern Speak?' In *Marxism and the Interpretation of Culture*. Urbana: University of Illinois Press.

Standing, Guy. 2011. *The Precariat: The New Dangerous Class*. London: Bloomsbury Academic.

Stickney, Anne. 2014. 'World of Warcraft up to 7.8 Million Subscribers'. *WoW Insider*.

Stiglitz, Joseph E. 2013. *The Price of Inequality*. New York: W. W. Norton & Co.

Strathern, Marilyn. 1992. 'Foreword: The Mirror of Technology'. In *Consuming Technologies: Media and Information in Domestic Spaces*, edited by Roger Silverstone and Eric Hirsch. London and New York: Routledge.

Stromberg, Peter. 1990. 'Elvis Alive? The Ideology of American Consumerism'. *Journal of Popular Culture* 24(3): 11–19.

Therborn, Göran. 2013. *The Killing Fields of Inequality*. Cambridge: Polity.

Van Vught, Frans. 2009. 'The EU Innovation Agenda: Challenges for European Higher Education and Research'. *Higher Education Management and Policy*, 21(2): 13–34.

Voinovich, Vladimir. 1988. *Moscow 2042*. London: Cape.

Voltaire. 2006. *Candide and Other Stories*. Oxford and New York: Oxford University Press.

Von Mises, Ludwig. 2005. *Liberalism: The Classical Tradition*. Indianapolis: Liberty Fund.

Wallace, David Foster. 1998. *A Supposedly Fun Thing I'll Never Do Again: Essays and Arguments*. London: Abacus.

Warwick, K. 2004. *I, Cyborg*. Urbana: University of Illinois Press.

Weil, Simone. 1963. *Gravity and Grace*. London: Routledge and Kegan Paul.

Weil, Simone. 2001. *Oppression and Liberty*. London: Routledge.

Wertheim, Margaret. 2013. 'Physics's Pangolin'. *Aeon Magazine* (June).

Žižek, Slavoj. 1989. *The Sublime Object of Ideology*. London: Verso.

Index